# Honor Your Father

BroadStreet Publishing Group, LLC
Racine, Wisconsin, USA
www.broadstreetpublishing.com

HONOR YOUR *Father*

## ○ RESET

*My Family Legacy*

Copyright © 2016 Great Commandment Network

ISBN–13: 978-1-4245-5125-5 (hardcover)
ISBN–13: 978-1-4245-5126-2 (e-book)

Cover by Chris Garborg at www.garborgdesign.com
Interior by Kimberly Sagmiller at www.fudgecreative.com

Stock or custom editions of BroadStreet Publishing titles may be purchased in bulk for educational, business, ministry, fundraising, or sales promotional use. For information, please e-mail info@broadstreetpublishing.com.

Printed in China
16 17 18 19 20 5 4 3 2 1

SPIRIT-
EMPOWERED
*Faith*

# HONOR
## YOUR
# *Father*

⭕ RESET

*My Family Legacy*

**BroadStreet**
PUBLISHING

# Contents

# SECTION 1

# SECTION 2

# SECTION 3

# SECTION 4

# SECTION 5

# APPENDIX:

*Preface*

L isten carefully and you will hear it...
The heart cry for fathers.

What is your heart longing for?

Your heart may long for a spiritual father or mentor. As a son or daughter, you may want to deepen or heal your relationship with your dad. As a father or mother, you may hope for improved family closeness. Or you may be a concerned individual who is burdened by the epidemic of fatherlessness in our generation.

The heart cry for fathers makes it clear: fatherlessness is one of the greatest social evils of a generation. The intensity of the heart cry helps determine our response: we must raise awareness that "dads matter" and that every child needs an intentional father or father figure.

The role of father was created by God and is irreplaceable. Since the glory of children is their fathers (Proverbs 17:6), and God commands his church to care for the fatherless (James 1:27), every child needs a loving and active father in his or her life.

Fathers are responsible before God to lead their families and spiritually train their children in the nurture and admonition of the Lord. Since fatherhood on earth is a representation of the eternal fatherhood of God, each father is called by God to be a faithful provider (Matthew 7:11; 1 Timothy 5:8), a strong protector (Matthew 2:13–14; Luke 11:21), a loving leader (Ephesians 6:1–4), a respectable authority (Hebrews 12:4–11), a truthful teacher (Deuteronomy 6:7; Proverbs 4:1–4), a living example (John 5:19–23; 1 Corinthians 11:1), and a compassionate friend (Psalm 103:13; John 15:15) to his children.

Let's face it. In an imperfect world with imperfect people, our family legacy may look different than the description above. In an imperfect world with imperfect people, how will our families thrive? How will our relationships flourish if our family legacy needs a reset? The good news is that our heavenly Father tells us where to start. The place to begin a reset of a family legacy has been carefully wrapped in a command from our Lord. Listen to His command and then be sure you hear the promise:

"Honor your father and mother, so that you may live long in the land the Lord your God is giving you." (Exodus 20:12 NIV)

The Fatherhood CoMission is committed to championing the role of fathers and desires to see the Lord turn the hearts of fathers to their children and the hearts of children to their fathers (Malachi 4:6). May dads be strengthened to live out the greatest of callings—father! May families see their legacy reset as they honor God and His Word!

Mitch Temple
Executive Director, The Fatherhood CoMission
www.honoryourfathertoday.com

## *Introduction*

Honor *Your Father* is designed to bring a fresh experience to fathers, families, and those who care about future generations. The goal of this resource is to empower fathers and families with a relational faith—a faith that transforms both a relationship with God and with other people.

In order to fully illustrate what a relational faith includes, we have defined forty different Spirit-empowered outcomes (see Appendix). Honor *Your Father* is written with a focus on five of these outcomes:

1. A Spirit-empowered faith experiences God as He really is, through deepened intimacy with Him.
2. A Spirit-empowered faith ministers His life and love to our nearest ones at home and to our extended family, and it includes faithful engagement in His body, the church.
3. A Spirit-empowered faith lives abundantly in "the present," as His Word brings healing to hurt, anger, fear, guilt, and condemnation, which are hindrances to abundant life.
4. A Spirit-empowered faith bears witness to a confident peace and expectant hope in God's lordship in all things.
5. A Spirit-empowered faith yields to the Spirit's protective cautions and transforming power to bring life change.

By highlighting and focusing on these outcomes, Honor *Your Father* hopes to serve the much-needed vision of a twenty-first-century spiritual awakening.

In response to the spiritual wake-up call on September 11, 2001, the Awakening America Alliance has been faithfully urging Christ's followers to gather for Cry Out America prayer gatherings across the nation, to engage in an annual rhythm of prayer, and to take action around twenty indicators of awakening (see www.awakeningamerica.us for more information). These indicators of awakening include:

- covenant marriage
- next gen discipleship
- care for children

This resource is designed to support this vision of spiritual awakening beginning with the closest of relationships—our family.

The *Honor Your Father* resource is a useful tool for any individual who wants to reset their family's legacy and begin a personal spiritual awakening within their marriage and family. *Honor Your Father* is also an important tool for pastors and church leaders who want to strengthen the families of their congregation and usher in a spiritual awakening in a community. What might change in a church and a community if small groups gathered together to celebrate fathers? What impact might there be if an entire sermon series helped a congregation learn how to reset their family legacy? Imagine what could be different if thousands of churches, with millions of fathers and families, took seriously the biblical admonition to honor fathers and live as fathers worthy of honor!

# RESET

## A PRAYER TO BRING HOPE

## RESET YOUR FAMILY LEGACY

When your computer or mobile device freezes, you know to hit the reset button. A reset restores the system to its original design. Hitting *reset* gives it a fresh start. So what happens when it's something in your life that feels frozen? Do you ever wish you could start over? Everyone feels that at times. And Jesus is the reset. Jesus restores you to your original design. He gives you a fresh start. That's what we hope this resource does for your family legacy. May it be a fresh start in your relationship with Jesus!

The *Honor Your Father* resource is intended to serve the Reset Movement. Reset is a work of anyone and everyone who wants to see Jesus bring hope to this generation and to this nation. Reset began as a prayer and dream of a young leader from North Dakota named Nick Hall, to see this generation unite around Jesus. The vision was never about one person or organization but a partnership around Jesus—and Jesus calls everyone.

Reset is not an organization. Reset is a prayer and a movement of people sharing the message of the hope Jesus brings when we pray it. The vision is not to facilitate a passive audience,

---

but to catalyze an army of individuals who are actively praying to Jesus to reset their lives, their communities, and their cities—and actively seeking to live a life reset by Jesus. While there are organizations involved, the fuel of this movement is you.

The Reset Movement has identified four ways to start your reset. These four ingredients are the inspiration for the calls to action we have inserted into each of the writings by the authors in this resource.

 **LEARN** to Encounter Jesus

 **PRAY** and Experience Scripture

 **SHARE** with Others in Community

 **LOVE** Others in Community

The message of Reset is that Jesus can and will reset your life. And that same message and invitation is shared at Reset events. The events are a place to connect in person with others who are praying and living reset lives, hear stories of what Jesus is doing, and celebrate Jesus with hundreds and thousands of others who are praying for a reset. Go to www.resetmovement.com for more information.

Finally, The Great Commandment Network is thrilled to serve each contributor and ministry partner through this resource. Our resource development and training team serves various partners as they develop Spirit-empowered disciples who walk intimately with God's Son, God's Word, and God's people. May Jesus richly bless the unity, commitment, and faith that *Honor Your Father* represents.

Terri Snead
Executive Editor, Great Commandment Network

**The Great Commandment Network** is an international collaborative network of strategic kingdom leaders from the faith community, marketplace, education, and caregiving fields who prioritize the powerful simplicity of the words of Jesus to love God, love others, and see others become His followers (Matthew 22:37–40; Matthew 28:19–20).

great commandment ♥net

# SECTION 1

# PREFACE: HONORING YOUR HEAVENLY FATHER

*What does the Lord your God require of you?
He requires only that you fear the Lord
your God, and live in a way that pleases him,
and love him and serve him with all your heart
and soul. And you must always obey the
Lord's commands and decrees that
I am giving you today for your own good.*
(Deuteronomy 10:12–13)

## A SPIRIT-EMPOWERED FAITH

experiences God as He really is through deepened intimacy with Him. Let these authors encourage your Spirit-empowered faith:

- The Father Figure—Josh McDowell
- A Heavenly Father We Can Relate To—Mark Williams
- Honoring the Real God to Honor Your Father—Jade Lee
- Reconciling the Lamb with the Lion—Sammy Rodriguez

# THE FATHER FIGURE

From *The Father Connection*
by Josh McDowell

## JESUS, RESET MY FAMILY LEGACY

*Jesus, remind me often of the kind of Father
that You are to me. I want to have fresh,
frequent experiences of Your love for me so
that I can share that love with others.*

## PREFACE

The nature and character of our Father in heaven reveals that a
godly father is one who comforts and supports his children in
life's trials and difficulties. The Bible says, "The righteous cry out,
and the LORD hears them; he delivers them from all their troubles.
The LORD is close to the brokenhearted and saves those who are
crushed in spirit" (Psalm 34:17–18 NIV).

Our Model Father is the Father of compassion and the God of all
comfort. He responds to our crises and calamities, not with impa-
tience and indignation but with comfort and support. He knows
that it helps immensely in times of difficulty to have someone on
whom we can rely and someone in whom we can find strength
(2 Corinthians 1:3–4).

God's comfort extends to "all our troubles." He comforts and supports us when we suffer persecution for His name's sake and when we suffer the consequences of our own foolish behavior. He comforts us when we deserve it least, when we're slogging through a mess of our own making. He supports us when we are weak, and He comforts us when we fall.

Our Father is comforting and supporting even when He must discipline us. The psalmist David wrote, "Your rod and your staff, they comfort me" (Psalm 23:4). The shepherd's staff was used as an instrument of comfort and support, lifting newborns, drawing lambs closer, and guiding sheep through dangerous or difficult routes. The rod, on the other hand, was an instrument of defense and discipline. It was used to deter or subdue attackers and for correcting wayward or recalcitrant members of the flock. Both instruments, however—the staff and the rod—were sources of comfort to the psalmist because both were wielded by a compassionate and supportive Shepherd.

 **PRAY and Experience Scripture**

*Give thanks to the LORD, for He is good.* (Psalm 107:1 NIV)

Reflect for a moment on one of the rods of correction the Shepherd uses in our lives: the Ten Commandments. What was God's motive when He gave the Ten Commandments to Moses and the children of Israel and eventually to us? Why did He give commandments such as "Honor your father and mother"?

God undoubtedly gave the Ten Commandments in order to provide testimony of His character, to portray righteous living, and to clarify sin's darkness, but we must look deeper in order to see the Father's heart. Our heavenly Father also gave the Ten Commandments because He knew how deeply sin would hurt us. Like a loving parent would warn a child not to touch a hot stove, God's heart of love is what motivated Him to establish rules and commandments (Deuteronomy 10:13). Out of a desire for our protection, God intended the commandments to be like "stop signs" for our behavior because He knows that when we violate them, we experience hurt. Remember some of the commands from Scripture and hear them from a Father who doesn't want us to experience hurt. Exodus 20:13–15 (NIV) reminds us:

- You shall not murder.
- You shall not commit adultery.
- You shall not steal.

How do you feel toward your heavenly Father as you reflect on His compassionate, protective motive?

*As I consider the loving motive behind God's gift of His commandments, I feel…*

*I'm filled with thanks because of God's heart for my good and His desire to protect me, because of how He…*

Plan to share your responses with your prayer partner or a small group.

God's commands are clear. His motive is love. But how does the Father respond when we choose to ignore His commands? Romans 5:8 tells us: "But God showed his great love for us by sending Christ to die for us while we were still sinners." Even when we sin, the Father's heart is compassionate, still loving. God isn't moved with vengeance or retribution when we disobey His commands. Instead, His heart grieves when our sinful choices cause us pain.

That's the kind of father we should want to be. By the supernatural presence and power of God's Holy Spirit living in us and working through us, we can reflect our Father's nature, comforting and supporting our children in all their troubles.

It is easy, of course, to comfort your daughter when she comes home from school disappointed because she got a B on a test instead of an A. It is easy to support your son when he had a less-than-stellar game on the soccer field. It's easy to comfort a child who's just fallen off a bike. But it's not so easy to offer comfort and support when they wreck the car because of a silly stunt or when they fail a test because they haven't studied. Those kinds of struggles—the ones they bring upon themselves—make it more difficult to respond in a godly way. But it is precisely at those times that our children most need to feel our comfort and support.

We can learn how to show the image of our Father by comforting and supporting our children, learning new ways to conform to His likeness. Here are ways to do that:

## Accept Your Limitations

One of the keys to becoming fathers who comfort and support their children is understanding and accepting our limitations. We can't prevent our kids from skinning their knees, but we can be there to pick them up and kiss their hurts. We can't stop our kids from making mistakes, but we can be there to help them correct their mistakes. We can't fix everything that goes wrong in their lives, but we can cheer them on when they succeed and lift them up when they fail.

## GAUGE THEIR NEEDS

A father who wishes to offer comfort and support to his children needs to be sensitive to their needs. Listen closely to what they say. Observe what they do. But don't stop there. Try to gauge what feelings and needs those words and actions reflect. A child who says, "You never do anything with me," may be expressing a need for a father's attention. A child who looks to the bleachers before stepping up to home plate may be looking for approval. A child who throws a temper tantrum when she fails may be crying out for comfort.

## LEARN WHAT COMFORT IS AND WHAT IT IS NOT

There are certain things a kid does not need when he or she is afraid or embarrassed or disappointed or hurting. Our children don't need advice when they hurt: "You know, your mistake was …" or "You know why this happened, don't you?" Our children may need correction, but not as the first response they receive ("Let this be a lesson to you"), nor do they always need instruction ("This can really build your character, if you let it"). Similarly, when a child is hurting, they don't need our inspiration ("Cheer up! It could be a lot worse, you know").

Sometimes, of course, it's quite necessary to offer discipline or correction when a young person is suffering the consequences of their own misconduct, but discipline will be much more effective when a father first offers comfort and support.

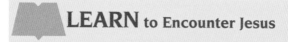

# LEARN to Encounter Jesus

*Praise be to the God and Father of our Lord Jesus Christ, the Father of compassion and the God of all comfort, who comforts us in all our troubles, so that we can comfort those in any trouble with the comfort we ourselves have received from God.* (2 Corinthians 1:3–4 NIV)

Where do we learn to comfort? Since God is the God of all comfort, we learn from Him. Pause right now and remember a time when you felt some measure of sorrow, sadness, discouragement, or disappointment of your own. Remember a time when either no one knew or no one cared that you were hurting. Can you remember a particular time of aloneness, either recently or in the distant past?

*I remember a particular time of sadness/aloneness when...*

Now, reflect further on this occasion of aloneness. As you recall this time when you were saddened, disappointed, or discouraged, what was Jesus feeling? And more specifically, what was He feeling for you? Scripture confirms that Jesus was actually hurting for you and caring about your pain.

Pause for a moment to reflect on Jesus. Picture Him sitting beside you. As the two of you talk together, Jesus reminds you that His heart is moved with compassion just for you. He reminds you how His heart was sorrowed by Israel's pain, how "in all their affliction He was afflicted" (Isaiah 63:9 NASB). And since Jesus is the same yesterday, today, and forever, He feels this same emotion for you (Hebrews 13:8). In all your affliction or hurt, He hurts.

Christ was afflicted and saddened when He saw you and the sorrow you experienced. He wants you to know: *My heart hurts when you hurt. I am moved with compassion when I see you hurting.*

Receive His comfort for you and then give Him thanks:

*God, thank You for being a God who has compassion for me. I'm especially grateful because...*

Now ask the Lord to help you express compassion for your children and your loved ones when they are hurting and alone.

## ENTER THEIR WORLD

If you really want your kids to feel your comfort and support, try entering their world. Make it your mission to discover what they're interested in right now, what they think is cool, what they enjoy, what kind of friends they're hanging around with. A father who truly wants to reflect the image of the Father of compassion, the God of all comfort, must take time for his children.

Many of us dads expect our kids to communicate with us on our level. We expect them to do things that interest us, yet we seldom or never enter into their interests and communicate at their level.

Offering these gifts to your children will have a long-reaching effect, both on them and on you. You'll be able to watch them stand up to unhealthy peer pressure, confident that they can find ample support and comfort when needed in their own home. You'll see them develop healthy friendships in which they are able not only to receive but to give as well. You will observe them—more and more as they grow—earning the respect and admiration of their peers (and of yours) as they become capable, confident young men and women who know they can rest secure in the care of their father.

 **SHARE** with Others in Community

*Let us consider how to stimulate one another to love and good deeds.* (Hebrews 10:24 NASB)

The writer of Hebrews reminds us that we all need encouragement when it comes to loving one another with specific actions. Think about your most precious relationships. Which of the good deeds below are you living out? Which ones could be improved? Make plans to share your responses with a prayer partner or small group.

- What have I recently done for fun with the most special people in my life?
- How am I doing at finding focused time with each individual child?
- Are the times I spend with my family drawing us closer or moving us apart?
- When have I recently verbalized my love, my interest in their world, shown involvement in my children's activities, and cared about their joys and pain?
- How might I better move beyond offering correction and advice in order to express more of His compassion?

The empowerment to love will only come as the Holy Spirit works in our lives, transforming us into the image of Christ. Take a few moments now and reflect on Christ's heart for your children and the other special people in your life.

 ## LOVE Others in Community

Review the list of questions above and how well you live them out with friends and family who don't know Jesus. Make plans to take initiative with one person in your sphere of influence.

# 2

# A HEAVENLY FATHER WE CAN RELATE TO

From *Lord, Teach Us to Pray*
by Mark Williams

> ## JESUS, RESET MY FAMILY LEGACY
> *Jesus, remind me often of the privilege You have to offer—that I can come to You in prayer and speak to You at any moment because You are my heavenly Father. Remind me what a blessing that is and how You deeply want to relate...to me!*

## PREFACE

Jesus taught that prayer is a matter of relationship. He said, "When you pray, say, 'Our Father, which art in heaven.'" Prayer is a relationship between Father and child. Truly productive and powerful prayer recognizes the fact that we, as believers, have truly been brought into the most powerful union in the world. We are in a relationship with the true and living God whereby we are the sons and daughters of God. Through the Holy Spirit, we have the privilege to call God *Abba* Father. It's the most intimate relationship in the world!

## WE'RE ADOPTED

We must realize that we "have received the Spirit of adoption, whereby we cry, *Abba*, Father." And His Spirit bears witness with our spirit that we are the children of God! We are heirs of God and joint heirs with Jesus Christ (Romans 8:15–17). Paul reminds us of the Father's perspective: "I will receive you, and I will be a Father to you, and ye shall be my sons and daughters, saith the Lord Almighty" (2 Corinthians 6:17–18). We have been brought into relationship! We have been brought near to Him by the blood of Christ. We are no longer strangers and foreigners, but fellow citizens with the saints and of the household of God! What a privilege to address God Almighty as "Our Father"! "Behold, what manner of love the Father hath bestowed upon us, that we should be called the sons of God" (1 John 3:1). When we enter into prayer we are to proclaim that relationship.

 **PRAY** and Experience Scripture

*Let all that I am praise the* Lord; *may I never forget the good things he does for me.* (Psalm 103:2 NLT)

Write out a special prayer of thanksgiving to God, praising Him for giving you a new sense of appreciation for who He is and how He is thrilled to be your loving heavenly Father. Let your prayer begin with words like:

*God, I praise You for the wondrous truth that You want to relate to me. You want to talk with me, and I am grateful because...*

*God, I praise You because it is a "good thing" that You have chosen to let me know You. That is especially amazing because...*

The Bible has a great deal to say about the fatherhood of God. Psalm 68:5 says, "A father of the fatherless, and a judge of the widows, is God in his holy habitation." Psalm 103:13 says, "Like a father pitieth his children, so the LORD pitieth them that fear Him." James 1:17 says that God is "the Father of lights, with whom there is no variableness, neither shadow of turning." Matthew 6:8b says, "Your Father knows what you have need of before you ask Him." And, verse 32 says, "Your Heavenly Father knoweth that you have need of all these things." And, in Matthew 7:11, "If ye then, being evil, know how to give good gifts unto your children, how much more shall your Father which is in heaven give good things to them that ask Him?"

These verses alone tell us much about the fatherhood of God. God is a Father to the fatherless—to orphans and to those who only had fathers who abused and neglected them. God is a God of compassion, One who pities His children, and One who shows sympathy, kindness, tenderness, and love to His children. God is a God who never changes. He is dependable. He will never leave you. He will never forsake you. God is a Father who knows what you need and is anxious to meet your needs and give you the desire of your heart.

 **SHARE** with Others in Community

Pause for a few minutes and reflect on the majesty and greatness of the fatherhood of God. Which one of God's attributes (named above) is especially meaningful to you?

*It means a great deal that my heavenly Father is One who _____, because…*

One way we can honor our heavenly Father is to become more like Him. Which one of God's attributes do you need to display more often? Do you need to:

- have more compassion, kindness, or tenderness with your children or family?
- display more dependability or keep your promises more often?
- be more sensitive to your children's/family's needs?
- be less selfish — thinking more of others' needs and less of your own?
- have a more giving heart toward the needs of your loved ones?

Talk with your prayer partner or small group about these needed areas of growth, and then pray together.

*Lord, change me and help me become more like You. With the power of Your Holy Spirit, make me more…*

Yes, God is sovereign, absolute, and independent, reigning as Jehovah Sabaoth in majestic glory. Yes, God is transcendent, infinitely exalted, and morally perfect, working all things after the council of His own will. But while God is transcendent, He is also imminent. He is the Great I AM! He is our Father. He is our Father who is in heaven. He is accessible. He is available. He is within your reach. He loves you with an everlasting love!

You don't have to be shy, bashful, or reticent about coming into His presence. He is your Father. The gate is unlocked. The door is open. The light is burning. The robe is pressed. The shoes are shined. The banquet table has been prepared. He is waiting on you with arms wide open. Come into His presence and proclaim your relationship.

Our Father, which art in heaven…

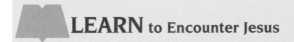

## LEARN to Encounter Jesus

*Just as you and I are one—as you are in me, Father, and I am in you.* (John 17:21 NLT)

*Come to me…* (Matthew 11:28 NLT)

Quiet your heart and focus for a few minutes on Jesus. Let this be a moment of personal encounter between you and the Savior. Because Jesus reminds us that He and the Father are one, we know that He is the perfect expression of our heavenly Father. So picture the face of Jesus as He stands before you with outstretched arms. He makes a personal invitation just for you. *Come to Me. I want to relate to you. I am available to you. I am accessible. I am within your reach, and I long for closeness with you. Pure and simple: I love you.*

Now honor Him with the response of your heart.

*Jesus, when I imagine how You long for me to be close to you, my heart is moved with* _____ *because…*

## → LOVE Others in Community

Ask the Lord to reveal a person in your life who needs to know the love of the Father. Plan to share a story of hope because of the relationship with your heavenly Father. Your words might begin with these:

*I am so grateful for the love of a heavenly Father who...*

*I know it sounds a little crazy, but He is an amazing Father to me because...*

# 3

## HONORING THE REAL GOD
## TO HONOR YOUR FATHER

An original article
by Jade Lee

### JESUS, RESET MY FAMILY LEGACY

*Jesus, remind me often of the love You have for me as my heavenly Father. Let my gratitude for how You love me empower me to strengthen and restore my relationship with my earthly father.*

### PREFACE

As we begin to ponder our need to honor God as our Father, it is hard not to think of our individual perspective of fatherhood. Our experiences with our earthly father most certainly inform our view of our heavenly Father.

### IMPRESSIONS OF FATHERHOOD

We each have personal images intricately tied to the tender yet powerful word *father*. For some, the visualization of *father* is an always-smiling, ready-to-embrace-you, tender man who instantly promotes feelings of joy and acceptance. Others remember the massive, outstretched hand that seemed to pull a never-ending supply of candy from his trouser pockets. There are also those who hear the word *father* and conjure up images of a scowling, rumpled brow and disappointed frown that seemed to cut the heart of a child desperately longing for expressions of his approval. And finally, there are others who may simply draw a blank when they try to visualize a father. As empty as a fresh pack of computer paper, no matter how many pages they turn, the landscape is full of empty memories. No calls, no visits, no talks with dad.

No matter what impression the word *father* has left upon our heart, we are reminded of its significant presence in the pages of Scripture. We are lovingly exhorted to honor our Father in heaven and fathers on this earth (Deuteronomy 5:16). But *how* do we honor our father? This question is inevitable when one out of every three American children live in a home where their biological father is not present.[1]

 **PRAY** and **Experience Scripture**

*Honor your father and mother, as the* Lord *your God commanded you....* (Deuteronomy 5:16 NLT)

Honoring your father includes fathers of all kinds: the attentive and neglectful, the kind and the abusive, the believers and the nonbelievers. The command is not conditional. Honoring your father requires faith to walk through the process of honoring. As you become an honoring person, you may be uncertain about your father's response, but you can have faith and confidence in your heavenly Father's pleasure.

---

1    James Nye, "1 in 3 children in the U.S. live without their father as number of two-parent households falls by 1.2m in ten years," DailyMail.com, December 26, 2012, http://www.dailymail.co.uk/news/article-2253421/1-3-US-children-live-father-according-census-number-parent-households-decreases-1-2-million.html.

And finally, honoring your father presupposes intimacy with God. Fulfilling the command to honor your father will be impossible in your own strength. Only as you yield to the Holy Spirit will you find the prompting and power to truly honor.

Pray a prayer of humility. First, tell God about your willingness to obey His command to honor your father. Next, tell God about any hesitancy you have about showing honor to your earthly father. And finally, declare your reliance on the Holy Spirit.

*God, I am committed to obeying Your Word, every part of it. You've commanded me to honor my father and mother, so I want You to know that I...*

*I yield to Your command and at the same time, I am going to need Your help because...*

*I am going to need Your Spirit to help me by...*

How to honor our father is a loaded question. Therefore, we must venture back to ask, "Why should we honor our father?" before we can answer the first. As Christians, we desire to live our life based on the truth of God's Word. The Bible is our standard and foundation. When we wonder *why* we should honor our earthly fathers, we must first return to the Word of God and how it describes the perfect, admirable love of our heavenly Father.

Honoring the real God is the first step toward honoring our earthly fathers. And honoring God is easy when we are freed from any vision of a harsh, "finger-pointing" God and begin to see a gentle, loving Father. Our hearts are enamored by His unconditional love the more our knowledge of who He is increases. And the more we come to know the true character of our heavenly Father, the more freedom we have as we look at our earthly fathers.

## THE GOOD, GIFT-GIVING FATHER

Our heavenly Father is one of the three persons of the Trinity—the Father, Son, and Holy Spirit. First Corinthians 8:6 reveals that "to us there is but *one God, the Father*, of whom are all things, and we in him; and one Lord Jesus Christ, by whom are all things, and we by him." God affectionately enters our world with a term we all can relate to on some level, choosing to introduce Himself to humanity as Father. He says, "Which of you, if your son asks for bread, will give him a stone? Or if he asks for a fish, will give him a snake? If you, then, though you are evil, know how to give good gifts to your children, *how much more will your Father in heaven give good gifts to those who ask him*?" (Matthew 7:9–11). Our heavenly Father is a good parent, a loving and attentive Father.

## LEARN to Encounter Jesus

"*And while he was still a long way off, his father saw him coming. Filled with love and compassion, he ran to his son, embraced him, and kissed him.*" (Luke 15:20 NLT)

Ask the Holy Spirit to remind you of the story of the prodigal son, but ask Him to refresh your experience of the Father in this well-known story. Read Luke 15:11–32, where the son demands his inheritance, lives a life of foolish choices, and then out of complete desperation and regret returns home to his father. Notice the father's response. While the son was a long way off, the father saw him coming. Imagine the scene of a father who sits on the front porch, scanning the horizon, looking for any sign of his son returning home. You have a Father like that. He can't wait to be with you, can't wait to run off the front porch and embrace you. Pause for a moment and imagine the scene of the story, but this time, imagine Jesus running out to meet *you*. He is filled with love and compassion. He runs to you and embraces you because His heart is thrilled to call you His child.

What does it do to your heart to imagine a God who can't wait to be with you? Tell the Father about your gratitude:

*Heavenly Father, when I imagine that You are scanning the horizon because You can't wait to be with me, I feel...*

*When I imagine that You are running to meet me and embrace me with a heart of love and compassion, my heart is moved with gratitude because...*

God describes Himself as a positive, providing Father who joyfully wants to give us good gifts. The good news is that no matter what sin and separation has occurred between us, the power of the gospel reconciles us back to our Father and back into intimate relationship. If we have no context of "father" or if we have an inaccurate view of fathers, we now can learn about fatherhood through intimate conversation with God and the revelation of Scripture. We can be filled with the "good gifts" from the Father in heaven, even gifts that we may have missed in our formative years.

What kind of gifts might our heavenly Father provide to His children? What kind of gifts are in store for those who are called to be His children? The Father's gifts include the meeting of all our physical needs, spiritual needs, and even the relational needs of our lives. God provides his children the gifts of: acceptance, approval, appreciation, respect, comfort, security, support, attention, affection, and encouragement. The Father gives us all of these through the abundance of His multifaceted grace (see 1 Peter 4:10).

God's love for us as our heavenly Father and our perspective of Him as a good, gift-giving dad prepares us to be restored to our earthly fathers. As our hearts are healed of pain through the love of God our Father, we are prepared to honor our natural father. Our dad, however imperfect, can be honored as we reflect on our heavenly Father.

 **SHARE** with Others in Community

*Whatever is good and perfect is a gift coming down to us from God our Father....* (James 1:17 NLT)

Talk with a prayer partner or small group about a "good gift" that has come from the Father to your life. Our gratitude for having received from our heavenly Father can reassure and empower our relationship with our natural father. Share your response to the following:

*Recently, I've been especially grateful for God's gift of _____ in my life. He is a tremendous Father because He has given...*

*My gratefulness for my heavenly Father's good gifts reassures me about my relationship with my earthly father because...*

## Healing a Hardened Heart

It is very hard to honor our fathers, God, or anyone else when our hearts have been hardened. This reminds us of a biblical character named Pharaoh. The Bible says Pharaoh's heart was hardened against God (the Father). The missing element in Pharaoh's life was honor. He failed to yield, to give respect, or to honor the God of the Israelites. Pharaoh eventually gave honor to the Lord, but it was at his own expense.

When our hearts become hardened due to life's difficulty or pain, we must remember that honor is a choice. We don't have to remain forever calloused. Multiple times in my own relationship with my father, the Lord has convicted me about three acts of love. He has asked my hardened heart to express love as I forgive, confess, and restore.

I've had to forgive my father, confess that I was wrong for holding anger and resentment against my dad, and then make a commitment to restoring him back to his rightful place in my life. This process has not always been easy, but in return for my obedience, I've seen my father travel for hours just to kneel at my feet, weeping words of godly sorrow.

It was through my place of humility that God brought healing, restoration, and the healthy relationship I desired. He wants to do the same for each of us as we listen to His leading. In fact, He promises to give us a softened, loving heart if we receive by faith, saying, "I will give you a new heart and put a new spirit in you; I will remove from you your heart of stone and give you a heart of flesh" (Ezekiel 36:26).

So go and be bold; don't be afraid to exemplify love, because you will be glad you took a step of faith. Even if your father does not respond the way you desire, you will be able to say you have

obeyed a very important part of God's Word, and your heavenly
Father will always be there to carry you.

 **LOVE** Others in Community

*That it may go well with you in the land the* LORD *your God is giving
you.* (Deuteronomy 5:16 NIV)

Ask the Holy Spirit to prompt you with any needed areas
of change in your life. Ask Him:

- *Is my heart hardened? Do I need more humility or a new
  heart from You?* (Ezekiel 36:26)
- Is there any forgiveness that You want me to show
  to my father?
- *Is there anything that I need to confess to You or to my
  earthly father? Search me, Lord, and know my heart...*
  (Psalm 139:23).
- *Is there any restoration needed in my relationship with my
  father?*

Ask the Holy Spirit to reveal the answers, and then make
plans to live out anything He reveals.

Talk to others who don't know Jesus about the transfor-
mational power of our heavenly Father.

# 4

## RECONCILING THE LAMB WITH THE LION
From *The Lamb's Agenda*
by Sammy Rodriguez

### JESUS, RESET MY FAMILY LEGACY
*Jesus, I want to live a life that is both humbly submitted to You and boldly proclaiming of Your powerful love. I want to live in the freedom of Your forgiveness and share Your forgiveness with others.*

### PREFACE

The lion has one real enemy in the animal world: rival lions that want what he has. In captivity, male lions often live more than twenty years. In the wild, they are lucky to live as long as ten. The wild is a brutal place.

### THE LION ROARS

One afternoon, I happened to catch a television special on the subject of lions. A lion that had just come back from a hunt returned brutally and mortally wounded. He barely managed to return to his camp, scarred and bleeding. The narrator let us know the outlook was grim. "The proud king of the jungle now stands wounded without strength to raise his head, lift up his paws and claws, or even open up his eyes."

Amidst his "pride"—an apt name for the cubs and lion-esses who depended on him—the wounded lion sat waiting for the inevitable. With a sense of triumph, the same enemies that ambushed the lion returned to serve a final blow. As the ene-mies drew closer and began their assault, the same wounded lion that could not raise his head or lift his paws suddenly breathed a sound. It seemed faint at first, but it surged and turned into a savage snarl and then a full-throated roar of the sort that night-mares are made of. With some accuracy, Proverbs 30:30 describes the lion as "mighty among beasts, who retreats before nothing." Immediately and without exception, the startled enemies of this lion fled into the wilderness, leaving the cubs unharmed and food uneaten. The narrator captured it best when he said, "The ene-mies of the lion know very well that as long as the lion can roar, they cannot take away what belongs to him!"

There are times when a Christian, too, must be a lion. Yet, as much as we might admire them, we cannot be like the lions in the wild. We have a double obligation. We are called to defend the cross and how it impacts our human relationships with, when necessary, a lion's roar. And yet, at the same time, we are asked to embrace the metaphorical motif embodied in the simplicity of the lamb—humility, gentleness, and submission. The lambs and the sheep know the shepherd's voice. As such, we stand with great humility and submission as the Good Shepherd guides us through the pastures of life. "I am the good shepherd; I know my sheep and my sheep know me," we learn in John 10:14–15, "just as the Father knows me and I know the Father—and I lay down my life for the sheep."

# SHARE with Others in Community

*You must not have any other god but me.* (Exodus 20:3 NLT)

*Honor your father and mother. Then you will live a long, full life in the land the LORD your God is giving you.* (Exodus 20:12 NLT)

To honor is to show abundant, merited respect, to affirm great worth and value. We have a "vertical" command to honor and affirm the great worth of our heavenly Father. We have a "horizontal" command to honor our earthly father. Sometimes it may seem as if the two commands conflict with each other. Talk with a prayer partner or small group about your reflections on the sentences below:

*God commands me to honor Him and respect Him. I have no struggle with that when it comes to...*

*I do struggle to honor God with...*

*When it comes to my relationship with my earthly father, there have been times when it has been hard to honor him because...*

# PRAY and Experience Scripture

*Search me, O God, and know my heart; test me and know my anxious thoughts. Point out anything in me that offends you.* (Psalm 139:23–34 NLT)

Lions roar when we share His forgiveness. Forgiveness is often one of the most challenging topics for a Christ follower to reconcile. It's often difficult to submit to the vertical command to forgive while the lion inside of us longs for justice and restitution. As Jesus followers who are committed to roar like lions and live like lambs, we must forgive those who have disappointed or hurt us in the past, because we know that to receive the forgiveness of God means extending the forgiveness to others.

Pray now and ask God to search your heart and test you. Ask Him if there is any area of unforgiveness that needs to be addressed in your life—ask Him to point out anything that offends or hurts Him.

*God, I want You to search my heart and see if there is any struggle with forgiveness in me. Show me, Lord. I want to see and confess anything that offends You....*

## WE'RE TO BE BOTH LIONS AND LAMBS

As Christians, we are both lions and lambs: horizontal lions and vertical lambs. As lambs, we maintain a vertical silence of reverence and humility. We are not afraid to kneel, to submit ourselves to God's mercy, to lie down in his green pastures. As lions, let loose in a world of rival lions more savage than we can ever be, we nonetheless have an imperative to roar when enemies of our faith threaten our offspring and our culture. As lions, our responsibility is broad. No one anywhere, no matter what the nationality or the faith, is beyond our concern. The world is our pride. For many secular activists, roaring is easy enough. Say whatever comes to mind as loudly as you can say it and follow up with violence if it seems to help your cause. After all, in a world without God, as Fyodor Dostoyevsky famously said, "Everything is permitted." For a Christian, everything is not permitted. Our role as lion is tempered by our relationship with Christ. We have to ask ourselves at critical moments, "What would Jesus do?" We cannot forget our humility before God, our adherence to His law, and our commitment to the truth. Our roar cannot be one of confrontation and instigation, but must be one of revelation and reconciliation. Our roar must prompt the serpent, the wolf, and the fox to flee, but it must also shower them with truth and love, however unwanted. Our roar must convey a message that Christianity and the transformative message of righteousness and justice will never be silenced. Finally, our roar must clearly present the imagery of the One who was crucified a lamb and resurrected a lion. It is not at all easy to convey this kind of information and still roar, but roar we must.

## LEARN to Encounter Jesus

"But when you are praying, first forgive anyone you are holding a grudge against, so that your Father in heaven will forgive your sins, too." (Mark 11:25 NLT)

"If you forgive those who sin against you, your heavenly Father will forgive you. But if you refuse to forgive others, your Father will not forgive your sins." (Matthew 6:14–15 NLT)

Ask the Holy Spirit to show you an image of Jesus holding a beautifully wrapped gift for you. Jesus presents His gift of forgiveness and lays it at your feet. The gift is yours to receive. Jesus is delighted to grant this gift because He knows when you receive His forgiveness you'll have freedom from guilt and pain of the past. Jesus also knows that when you give the gift of forgiveness to another person, you are freed from anger and experience the healing that comes from His comfort. Talk to Jesus about your struggle to forgive.

*Jesus, I am struggling to forgive _____ because...*

*Remind me of the gift of forgiveness You have already given to me...*

*Because I have already received Your forgiveness for _____, I'm asking You to help me let go of my anger about...*

*Empower me to forgive _____, just as You have forgiven me.*

One finds some other useful words of wisdom in James 1:12: "Blessed is the one who perseveres under trial because, having stood the test, that person will receive the crown of life that the Lord has promised to those who love him." We all face trials. For the Christian lamb, with a proper understanding of his or her vertical alignment with God, trials present opportunities to grow in God's grace and in our own character. James said, "My dear brothers and sisters, take note of this: Everyone should be quick to listen, slow to speak and slow to become angry, because human anger does not produce the righteousness that God desires" (James 1:19–20).

## THE HORIZONTAL ROAR

Lions are featured heavily in Christian tradition. There are many references to lions in the Old Testament, and all of them suggest the relative power that the lion possesses. In Christianity's early centuries, of course, lions were more than metaphorical. To satisfy pagan gods and stimulate local passions, Christians were periodically fed to very real lions. That did not stop the early Christians. Indeed, their faith and fortitude in the face of death inspired others. These Christians continued to roar despite the threats. If they could do so, we have no excuse for staying silent here in North America. Typically, we fear little more than cold shoulders, angry e-mails, media slams, and the loss of tax exemptions, and yet that is often enough to keep many of us silent in the face of injustice and cultural degradation.

 **LOVE Others in Community**

Take a moment and consider how the Lord offers us community with Him as our Good Shepherd and communion with one another in the body of Christ. As His sheep, we are a part of His eternal flock. Now consider how you might fulfill the Great Commission and voice His message of the gospel. Who needs to hear your "roar"—to hear you proclaim the love of Christ in our world?

*Jesus, who needs me to boldly stand up and tell them about You and Your love?*

# SECTION 2

# PREFACE: THE PROMISED BLESSING OF HONORING YOUR FATHER

*So then, as we have opportunity,
let us do good to everyone, and especially
to those who are of the household of faith.*
(Galatians 6:10 ESV)

## A SPIRIT-EMPOWERED FAITH

ministers His life and love to our nearest ones at home and to our extended family, and it includes faithful engagement in His body, the church. Let these authors encourage your Spirit-empowered faith:

- Jesus Resets Families—Nick Hall
- Training Children to Honor Their Fathers—Barbara Doyle
- Honor as the Priority—Todd Stawser
- My Tribute—Mitch Temple

# 5

## JESUS RESETS FAMILIES

An original article
by Nick Hall

---

### JESUS, RESET MY FAMILY LEGACY

*Jesus, I want You to remind me often of how
You have chosen me to be a part of Your family.
Keep me mindful of the blessings that come from
You and help me remember to talk about You
with my own children and family.*

---

### PREFACE

When we ask Jesus for a reset, He does more than forgive our sins. He literally exchanges our family line for His own. Romans 8:14 reminds us: "For those who are led by the Spirit of God are the children of God" (NIV). The reality of a new family in Jesus is so much more incredible than a clean track record. God doesn't just look on our past and say, "I'm giving you hope for a new family in heaven." No—instead, He looks on us and says, "You are my child; I have reset your past, your future, and your present." God's call doesn't just change our future; it changes our today. It welcomes us into the family of God right now.

I can still see my grandparents on their knees, praying before they went to bed. I was only a child the first time I peeked in to get a glimpse of what had become something of legend in the Hall household. Each night, my mom's parents would kneel together to pray for every kid and grandkid by name. Do you think that had an impact on me?

I know it did. Prayer changes things.

My grandparents' prayers impacted my parents, aunts, uncles, cousins, and extended relatives. As a result of this legacy, my parents prayed with us regularly. My dad studied Scripture. My mom would put up Bible verses on my mirror, finding different ways to encourage us in our faith.

## When Your Family Legacy Needs a Reset

As I write this, I recognize most of us do not come from a legacy of faith. When I travel to speak for various events, my heart breaks at stories of brokenness at home. It's clear that this generation needs Jesus to reset their family legacy.

The good news is that all of us come into the family of God with a reset.

Hebrews 11, the great "Hall of Faith," is filled with stories of God resetting family legacies. Abraham, who was wealthy in his homeland, was called by God to leave everything he knew and venture into the unknown. Every Christian traces their legacy of faith back to Abraham.

Ruth, a Moabite foreigner, had a moment of decision when she could return to her homeland. Instead, she refused and chose to follow the God of the Israelites. That moment redefined her family legacy (all the way to King David and even Jesus!).

Rahab, a prostitute, is recorded in Hebrews 11 with spiritual giants like Moses and Abraham because she made a decision to follow the living God. Her past had no influence on her legacy because of the spiritual reset she received.

Whatever your background, whether you were raised in the church or near the local pub, there is hope when we trust in Jesus. In Jesus, we all experience a reset to our family legacy because we are adopted into His.

 **LEARN** to Encounter Jesus

*God decided in advance to adopt us into his own family by bringing us to himself through Jesus Christ. This is what he wanted to do, and it gave him great pleasure.* (Ephesians 1:5 NLT)

Pause for a few moments and slowly read the Scripture above. Make it personal. "God decided in advance to adopt *me* into his own family...and it gave him great pleasure!" Now imagine Jesus sitting beside you. He puts his arm around you and smiles with great pride as He explains, "Just think. The Father has chosen you to be a part of our family. As your heavenly Father, He wanted to provide for you, protect you, care for you, and guide you, so He sent Me to bring you to Himself. It gives Him great pleasure to see *you* as part of His family."

Allow the Holy Spirit to reaffirm the truth of this relationship and confirm your adoption into the family of God. Now express your thanks for God's amazing gift.

*Father, I am grateful You decided to adopt me into Your family, because...*

*I am amazed at what You went through to have me join Your family, and I thank You for...*

## A New Legacy

A few years ago I traveled with Winter Jam, the largest annual Christian music tour in the world. Each night, I would speak on 1 John 3:1, "See what great love the Father has lavished on us, that we should be called children of God! And that is what we are!" (NIV).

And every time, I was amazed at the response. People would come up to me, confessing their broken past and telling me what God had done in their lives that night.

Through each powerful story, I realized once again that we are all longing for that sense of belonging. We want more than money or popularity, more than Facebook friends and Instagram followers. All the treasure in the world is meaningless without someone to share it with, some cause worth living for. We all want parents who love and encourage us and siblings who stand by our side. Our families on earth were meant to be a reflection of heaven.

# PRAY and Experience Scripture

*I give you thanks, O LORD, with all my heart....* (Psalm 138:1 NLT)

Pause for the next few moments and give thanks to the Lord with all your heart. Thank Him for giving you a family and parents who have been your place of belonging, your source of encouragement and love. Or thank Jesus for being your place to belong, your source of encouragement and love. Take time to reflect and then give thanks to the Lord.

*Lord, I am thankful that You have given me a family who...*

*Lord, I am thankful that You are my source of _____ because...*

## Our Calling as Reset Families

I heard someone say once, "God doesn't have grandchildren; He only has sons and daughters." Yet God's invitation is that each generation would experience his reset and that we might gather as many families as possible for the great homecoming.

In Deuteronomy 6, immediately following the Great Commandment is the command to pass along the love of God and His teaching to the next generation.

*"These commandments that I give you today are to be on your hearts. Impress them on your children. Talk about them when you sit at home and when you walk along the road, when you lie down and when you get up. Tie them as symbols on your hands and bind them on your foreheads. Write them on the doorframes of your houses and on your gates."* (Deuteronomy 6:6–9 NIV)

In Joshua 4 we see the same thing. God miraculously stops the waters of the Jordan River to allow His people to pass over it on dry ground. When the people get over to the other side, God commands Joshua to order the people to build a monument.

*"In the future, when your children ask you, 'What do these stones mean?' tell them… These stones are to be a memorial to the people of Israel forever."* (Joshua 4:6–7 NIV)

The things that God has done in your past should be defining stories in your family legacy moving forward. Write down what God has done and tell the story!

I'm convinced that one of the most overlooked disciplines in the Christian life is that of remembering. Remembrance inspires us with a track record of God's faithfulness, inspiring us in turn to live lives of faith like our forefathers. This is the purpose of Hebrews 11—that we would see the example of saints laid before us and run hard after Jesus (Hebrews 12:1–2). Godly remembrance is meant to lead to action, so that the next generation can see and imitate bold faith.

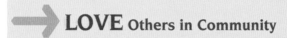

## LOVE Others in Community

Plan some moments when you tell your children, spouse, friends, and family about the times when God has provided for you, protected you, or rescued you. First remember these defining stories on your own and then share them with others.

*I remember how God provided for me/protected me/rescued me when...*

*I'm so grateful for how the Father showed up in my life when...*

*I plan to share these remembrances with _____ when...*

I want my family to experience "going after Jesus" together. I want my kids to taste and see that the Lord is good—that He still meets daily needs and has the power to heal today. But for this to happen, it needs to be more than simply going through the motions. This is inviting God to reset the way we see our families altogether. This is more than mealtime prayer, more than tradition, more than weekly church services—this is Jesus alive in our lives.

Whatever your family legacy, Jesus is the reset. Jesus changes everything. He isn't interested in changing only your eternity but also your daily life. If you are a child of God, you have incredible promises to live by. He made you for so much more than one-generational faith. When we abandon our agendas and follow Jesus, we leave a reset legacy of living faith for future sons and daughters in the kingdom of God.

 **SHARE** with Others in Community

Plan to share your story of how Jesus has begun to reset your family legacy. Your words might begin like this:

*I am amazed at how Jesus is changing our family. Because of Jesus, we...*

# 6

## TRAINING CHILDREN TO HONOR THEIR FATHERS

An original article
by Barbara A. Doyle

## PREFACE

Luke 9 is a rudimentary message meant for each sincere believer of Jesus: "Then he said to the crowd, 'If any of you wants to be my follower, you must turn from your selfish ways, take up your cross daily, and follow me. If you try to hang on to your life, you will lose it. But if you give up your life for my sake, you will save it'" (Luke 9:23–24 NLT).

## A GOLDEN TREASURE

In 1986, my dad and I started what became a thirty-year, ongoing dialogue on Luke 9:23–24. Literally, this passage came to flavor our conversations and thread throughout our discussion for decades. I even incorporated this Scripture passage into Dad's eulogy, when we said good-bye and celebrated his life. As great as God's provision was for our family, my father endured times of struggle and strife. These emotional and physical challenges kept our dialogue and fellowship fresh. It was through these conversations with my father that my children saw what my relationship with Pops was all about. They learned firsthand about the love and admiration I had for him. This impression is a golden treasure from God because it set my children's understanding about what honor looks like.

Honor is learned. It's a part of the "do on earth as it is in heaven" principle of our faith. Since we are in a war for the souls of our children, we need to prepare the way for them to learn the meaning of honor. The first and foremost preparation for learning how to honor is through praying Scripture. Tattered sheets of Bible verses still take up residence in my Bible. For years, I've printed out, dated, and scribbled my children's names alongside specific Scriptures, using these passages to guide my prayers for their life. Many times I would even give each child passages of Scripture around a certain theme and then let them share the verse that the Holy Spirit nudged them to read and pray through. It surfaced fresh and current conversations of the heart like nothing else. Even to this day, my children call me up to pray with and over them!

## PRAY and Experience Scripture

*I honor and love your commands.* (Psalm 119:48 NLT)

Take the next few moments and pray for your children. Ask the Holy Spirit to empower your child to honor and love the commands of God. Claim the promises that can come true for your children as they live their lives according to God's commands.

*Jesus, I pray for my child. I pray specifically that he/she would learn to honor You in...*

*I pray that he/she would come to honor, respect, and live out all the commands that You have given us. Help me to talk about how Your commands are for our good. Remind me often how Your ways are the best ways and then remind me to share those with my children.*

## MEALTIME MEMORIES THAT BUILD HONOR

Mealtimes together have been a family priority through all the years my husband and I have had children. This priority has been consistent, from the toddler years to teens and straight through to the present. One of my husband's consistent prayers is for us to be a family that encourages one another and builds each other up. Even the best of our communication can still be void of healthy, intentional encouragement. Families with teens get this! It just does not come naturally. The greatest gift of our mealtime hour comes when we pass around a bowl (ready with folded-up pieces of paper with our names written on them), pick a name, and pray for each other. The heart, the words, and the sincerity that pours out of our children's mouths, without exception, portray the most beautiful mastery of encouragement. This fruit clearly honors their Dad's instruction and his heart.

## THREE MORE ORDINARY STORIES OF HONORING

When I choose my husband's name from the bowl in our mealtime experience, or if I pray for the meal as we start, I will often interject: "And thank you Lord for Daddy, for his hard work, for

Your provision for our needs through him, and for all those You intend for him to interact with and bless today..." It seems natural to thank the Lord for the work He provides through Brian for our family. I had no idea how much it touched Brian's heart until one day when he shared specifically how much those words meant to him. My words modeled honor. They were an example of how to convey honor to my husband and show our children how to honor their father. And since women don't instinctively understand a man's thoughts and ways, I was so grateful that my husband was vulnerable with me.

 **SHARE** with Others in Community

*Be happy with those who are happy....* (Romans 12:15 NLT)

Make plans to talk to a prayer partner or small group about the times when you have felt honored, even in small ways. Rejoice and celebrate how God can provide through relationships. If you are married or have adult children, remember the times when your family members have said honoring words to you or about you. Be vulnerable and tell your family members how much it meant to hear these words.

*I really feel honored when someone says words like...*

*I experience respect and honor when someone...*

Other opportunities that I have seized to teach my children about expressing honor to their dad are his birthday, Father's Day, or Christmastime. It is not always a perfect event or presentation, but these occasions definitely provide a platform for our children to consider their father's interests, priorities, and values. This consistent challenge to consider their dad helps the children learn to honor their father in an observant, servant-hearted, thoughtful way. It is a chance for them to express their thankfulness and show creativity or generosity to him. Sometimes the children's honor is expressed in the words of a handmade card or a picture from their favorite memory, or they may even purchase a gift. These expressions of care and thoughtfulness have become a blessing over the years.

Modeling and teaching honor is not always an easy endeavor. My husband is not a man who gets uptight about things around the household. He is light spirited if there is a basket of laundry sitting around or if there is a sink of dirty dishes. He will roll up his sleeves and gladly pitch in to help. What *is* of high importance to him is punctuality. What a great quality! When I met Brian, he was teaching a workshop on time management and I was attending—I needed all the tips I could get! This shows you where I come from on the spectrum of punctuality. I completely get the others-centeredness and importance of punctuality; yet, being a global thinker and multitasker, even to this day I struggle with being on time. It is a discipline I have yet to master. Despite my struggles in this area, my children are being taught to honor others and the importance of punctuality through their father's model! And all I can say is, "Thank God for His grace!"

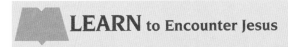

# LEARN to Encounter Jesus

*And this same God who takes care of me will supply all your needs from his glorious riches....* (Philippians 4:19 NLT)

Our God is a need-meeting God. He will supply all of your needs—sometimes directly through the Holy Spirit, and at other times, through the gift of the relationships He has ordained. Our role is to gratefully receive from His abundant supply—not demanding or dictating *how* the Lord might want to provide.

Imagine that Jesus is standing before you. Tell Him about your needs and share the tender places of your heart. Talk to Him about the places in your life that are still a struggle, relationships that are strained, or hopes that have gone unfulfilled. Now picture the person of Jesus. He stands before you and reminds you: "I am the Bread of Life. I am the God who takes care of all your needs. You can count on Me. Look for how I provide."

Claim the promise of God's provision and make your declaration of faith in Him.

*God, I need You to provide...*

*You've promised to provide all my needs, so I am trusting You to...*

*Thank You for being a God who cares about our needs...*

Honoring authority is not a norm in our culture. Authority itself is not even embraced, let alone honoring men, especially fathers. Countering this norm will be countercultural. Expect opposition. Proverbs 2:1–6 (NIV) says,

> My son, if you accept my words and store up my commands within you, turning your ear to wisdom and applying your heart to understanding, and if you call out for insight and cry aloud for understanding, and if you look for it as for silver and search for it as for hidden treasure, then you will understand the fear of the Lord and find the knowledge of God. For the LORD gives wisdom, and from his mouth come knowledge and understanding.

Just as we recognize the value of seeking biblical treasure, we must also actively recognize the importance of teaching our children to honor their fathers. This comes from the wisdom of God. Pursue this mission with all of your heart. Find methods that work for your family through feedback and daily observation. Teach your children to honor their father well so that they may live long in the land the Lord their God plans to give them (Exodus 20:12)!

# LOVE Others in Community

Ask the Holy Spirit to show you one individual (perhaps your spouse, family member, child, or friend) who could benefit from receiving more honor or respect. When the Lord reveals this person, ask them to respond to the following:

*I feel honored when...*

*It really feels respectful to me when someone says...*

After you hear their response, look for times and opportunities to meet their need for honor. Then talk about the God who deserves our honor and respect.

# HONOR AS THE PRIORITY

An original article
by Todd Stawser

## JESUS, RESET MY FAMILY LEGACY

*Jesus, help me reset the priority of showing honor.
Make me aware of the ways that I can demonstrate
more honor to You and to those around me.*

## PREFACE

The overwhelming message of Scripture for our relationships is love and honor. But when considering our elders, honor is lifted up as the priority for our relationships; it's the foundation from which a relationship will grow. We know God's fifth commandment and its clear call to honor our father and mother, but the appeal for honor must be emphasized to everyone who represents the older generation of our world. Scripture reminds us: "You shall stand up before the gray head and honor the face of an old man, and you shall fear your God: I am the LORD" (Leviticus 19:32 ESV). And: "Do not rebuke an older man...but exhort him as if he were your father..." (1 Timothy 5:1 NIV).

It's taken me a long time to learn what God desires of us in biblically honoring our fathers. As a little boy, I may have understood the meaning of obedience, but honor stood as an elusive unknown, nothing more than some archaic term reserved for kings or soldiers returning from war. While I endeavored to love my parents, honor remained a mystery, something I never knew how to express. Nevertheless, God quickly went to work.

Looking back at my childhood, I realize now that our family was providentially drawn to serve the elderly. Even from a young age, nursing home visitation was a weekly event. I saw glimpses of what it means "to honor" as we lived out God's plan for the elderly. Not only did our hearts turn to love these beloved seniors, but God's Word became a reality: "Pure and undefiled religion before God and the Father is this: to visit orphans and widows in their trouble" (James 1:27 NKJV).

Then, while still a young man with toddlers at home, God cast me into the end-of-life care for my mother-in-law and the in-home care of my father-in-law. Serving as a caregiver during those years quickly taught me that honor is only brought to bear through focused resolve. It is a treasure and a deep well of blessing that every man should pursue. My wife and I were drawn to the Word of God as we tried to understand the circumstances He had lovingly thrust us into. Through our caregiving journey, God revealed the true nature of biblical honor and its preeminence in the father-son relationship.

For me, the most impacting, critical lesson came from Christ himself. While our Lord hung on the cross, bearing the weight of our sin, His last exhortation was clear: "When Jesus therefore saw His mother, and the disciple whom He loved standing by, He said to His mother, 'Woman, behold your son!' Then He said to the disciple, 'Behold your mother!' And from that hour that disciple took her to his own home" (John 19:26–27 NKJV).

Hanging on the cross, with one remaining breath, Christ's priority was for his mother. He stopped to consider her. Jesus paused from the agony to remember her. And even amidst his enduring torture, the Savior ensured that his mother was cared for and loved the rest of her days. Men, this is honor.

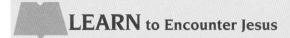

## LEARN to Encounter Jesus

Reflect for a few moments on the story mentioned above. Ask the Holy Spirit to allow you to sense the miracle of this moment in history.

Jesus looked down from the cross and, in the midst of excruciating pain, demonstrated concern for Mary. No amount of suffering or personal inconvenience prevented Christ from seeing His mother's need and taking initiative to meet it. He wasn't too preoccupied. He wasn't too busy. Jesus knew that Mary would need provision and care when He died, so Christ commissioned John to take care of Mary and provide for her needs.

And now imagine this: Because Jesus is the same— yesterday, today, and forever, you can rest assured that He sees your need. He's not too busy or preoccupied to notice your need. He sees that you need His care. Jesus notices when you have a need and will take action to meet it.

Pause and allow the Holy Spirit to plant this truth deeply into your heart and Spirit. Then pray a prayer of gratitude:

*Jesus, when I reflect on Your character and how You can't wait to meet my needs, my heart is moved with...*

*Jesus, I am grateful that You notice my needs and care about my life because...*

## STEPS IN THE RIGHT DIRECTION

Since learning these precepts of honor, I've enjoyed years of helping men successfully grow to honor their fathers. However, very often men will tell me, "I can't. I have no relationship with my dad!" Before I tell you where to begin, let me first share with you the key principle to giving honor. Without it, your efforts to honor will be feeble and even insincere.

Any effort to honor our *earthly* father must begin with a life devoted to honoring our *heavenly* Father. Honor starts by fearing God and recognizing that we can only love others because of God's sacrificial love for us through His Son, Jesus Christ: "Beloved, let us love one another, for love is of God; and everyone who loves is born of God and knows God" (1 John 4:7 NKJV).

It is through the recognition of our frailty and utter dependence on Christ that we're enabled to love others, speak words of life, and truly convey honor to another person. Before making any attempts to honor others, first take spiritual inventory of your heart and relationship with God.

### PRAY and Experience Scripture

*By humility and the fear of the Lord are riches, honor, and life.* (Proverbs 22:4 NKJV)

Reflect back on the time when you first entered into relationship with Jesus. Do you remember desiring to please Him, to bring joy to Him? Wasn't there a longing to avoid displeasing Jesus? You didn't want to do anything that would damage your relationship.

When you think back on this time, did you desire to:

- put away certain attitudes, habits, or behaviors in your life?
- avoid certain activities, places, and acquaintances?
- meditate upon God's Word, pray, and worship with other Jesus followers?
- share your experience with Jesus with other people?

*As I think back upon my first years in my relationship with Jesus, I recall not wanting to displease Him by...*

Ask the Holy Spirit to give you a fresh and deepened motivation to yield to Jesus and increase your dread of displeasing Him.

*God, I want to humbly return to my first love for You and my desire to please You at all costs. Help me live with honor so that I can enjoy the riches You desire for me...*

Honoring your father can be challenging, and you may feel ill equipped. Honoring may even be something you're tempted to shy away from. It is through your identity in Christ whereby your fear of giving honor will be cast away and you'll receive God's power to truly bless. With our focus on God, He gives us *power*, *love*, and a *sound mind* to restore relationships and selflessly give honor (2 Timothy 1:7). Once established, we can take steps forward in faith toward honoring, even where a poor father-son relationship exists.

# SHARE with Others in Community

*Be humble, thinking of others as better than yourselves.* (Philippians 2:3 NLT)

Make plans to talk with a prayer partner or small group about your ability to honor your earthly father. Consider sharing your responses to the following:

*I've been reflecting on how well I've lived out God's command to honor my father and mother. I believe that I have honored my father in...*

*I sense that I need to grow in the area of honoring my dad concerning...*

While all men are in different places in honoring their parents, the key is simply to move in the "right direction" no matter how big or small the steps. Through prayer, faith in Christ, and a diligence to pursue the relationship, we've consistently seen men advance their relationships with their father through honor. Don't seek perfection on day one—just move toward "better" and pursue more demonstrations of honor at every opportunity.

**LOVE** Others in Community

Ask the Holy Spirit to reveal one person who could benefit from hearing about your growth journey of honoring your
father. Ask the Spirit to reveal this person's relational and
spiritual needs and how to meet them.

*Holy Spirit, show me one person who needs to hear about my jour-
ney of learning to honor my father. Show me the needs of this person
and how I can meet them.*

# 8

## MY TRIBUTE
An original article
by Mitch Temple

## PREFACE

Writing a tribute to your father is a tremendously impactful experience. Listen in as Mitch Temple tells a story of admiration and writes a tribute about his father. Read along and pause for each reflective moment. Let these reflective moments become your own letter of tribute to your dad.

## DADS ARE IMPORTANT

The Scripture reminds us to "honor your father and your mother, so that you may live long in the land the LORD your God is giving you" (Exodus 20:12 NIV). Unfortunately, many sons and daughters have never received the blessing of a father. Twenty-four million children live without their fathers today. Many dads have failed to step up to the plate and be the fathers that God hardwired them to be. Some have missed the mark because of bad choices, some because of selfishness, and some because they followed in the steps of their own fathers.

The story of my father, Dr. Winston Temple, is like many stories—insightful, personal, and challenging. It's captivating at times and quite boring at others. Nonetheless, his story is my story. It helped to shape me into the man and father that I am today. I am eternally grateful.

The beauty of my father's story is that it was real-life drama, lived out by an ordinary servant of the King. My dad was rich with incredible strengths that were tempered with human frailties. Dad's story is one of perseverance, trials, faith, and service in God's kingdom. His story is an absolutely beautiful example of what it means to be a great dad and lead a life worthy of honoring.

Dad was raised in the shadow of some of the most momentous eras in our nation's history: World War II, the Korean War, Vietnam, and the Cold War. Dad's father was a rough, hard, strong-willed master sergeant who served in World War II during the Pacific Campaign. Dad was raised in the harsh conditions of poverty, turmoil, conflict, and alcoholism, with occasional episodes of faith and spiritual experience. Dad was blessed with a mother who instilled in him the basic principles of life, core values seasoned with common sense, and godly character that would be passed on to several generations.

After working his way through college in the early 1960s, Dad was recruited to one of the fastest growing manufacturing corporations in the nation at the time. Within just a short period of time, Dad was promoted to key positions in the company. He was, without a doubt, on the fast track to success and making an incredible salary for a man his age. The company expected great things from my dad, but because of the tremendous turmoil of his childhood, Dad felt a calling from God to provide something more valuable than material things for his family. Dad once shared that he didn't know exactly what he needed to do to help his family go to heaven, but he knew it had something to do with being a servant. So Winston gave up his lucrative career to become a minister, a servant to many.

 ## SHARE with Others in Community

*Be happy with those who are happy.* (Romans 12:15 NLT)

Reflect back to your own childhood. What positive memory do you have about your father? What was one of the good times you remember with Dad? If you can, try to remember a time before the age of twelve when you felt especially loved, cared for, approved or appreciated by your father. You might remember a special birthday, specific words of praise or affection from your dad, a sports achievement that you celebrated together, or perhaps there was an enjoyable trip. Remember the specifics of this positive memory:

*I remember feeling especially loved by Dad when...*

*I remember a positive time with my dad when...*

*I remember him fondly when I think about...*

✝ Share this memory with a prayer partner or small group. Rejoice together about the happy memories you have of your dad and then prepare to use these same memories to write a tribute for your father.

With little experience and money, Dad stepped out in faith. He followed God's calling into the unknown world of full-time ministry. At that time, Dad's library consisted of two books: a Bible purchased with green stamps and a worn-out Bible concordance that was held together with electrical tape. My father had little knowledge, experience, or wisdom about the life of ministry, but what he had was a deep, passionate love for God, his family, and other people.

For half a century, my father served God and His people through the local church and then ultimately as a seminary educator and administrator. He influenced thousands of people. Many individuals were led to the Lord, and countless hungry and discouraged souls were fed at his table. There are missionaries on foreign soils today because of Dad's efforts, and secular leaders all over this country have been positively impacted by my father's life.

Dad constantly gave from the heart. I can remember as a child how our family would have guests for dinner for many evening meals. Sometimes my mother knew they were coming, and sometimes they would arrive unexpectedly. With any family dinner, we might enjoy the company of a destitute traveler or an abused mother and her children. These family meals taught me to feel compassion for others, to serve others, and to sacrifice. More than once, I remember Mom or Dad giving their last five dollars to a hungry seminary student.

Dad was certainly not flawless, but among his many attributes, he taught us to admit our weaknesses and learn from our mistakes. My father became a "cycle breaker" and ended some generational patterns that plagued our family. He persevered in the ditches of life and lived with faith and honor. Dad knew what it meant to struggle, to do without, to experience illness, to be persecuted for the cause of Christ, and not to feel the love of his earthly father. Dad even knew what it meant to experience the deepest of life's struggles when we lost my older brother in a car accident at the age of forty-four. Through all of these trials, my father manifested God's love to others. He put his hand to the plow almost fifty years ago, and despite the trials and suffering, he never looked back.

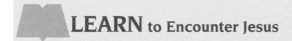 **LEARN** to Encounter Jesus

*Let the peace of Christ rule in your hearts....* (Colossians 3:15 NIV)

Reflect for a few moments on the areas where your father might have struggled. What were some of his weaknesses, and how did those weaknesses impact you? What hurts or painful moments did you experience in your relationship with your dad?

First, tell these to the God of all comfort. He wants to comfort your heart and bring you peace.

*God, I need Your comfort about...*

*A really painful time in my relationship with my father was when...*

*Please show me what You feel for me as you see me and the hurt I've experienced.*

Allow the Holy Spirit to comfort your heart. Let Him remind you that the God of all comfort can't wait to show you compassion (Isaiah 30:18). He hurts when you hurt; He weeps because you weep (see John 11:35–36). Allow the Comforter to comfort you.

After receiving comfort from God about the ways you have experienced hurt, you are now freer to honor your father with a grateful heart. Reflect on the character strengths and qualities you appreciate in your father.

I *appreciate my father for* _____ (his sense of humor, his diligence, the way he provided for our family, etc.)

Now, plan to include these insights in your written tribute to your father.

Dad went to be with the Lord on a cold November day in 2015. He fought a ten-year valiant battle against Parkinson's and heart disease. He was only seventy-four years old, but what a beautiful life he packed into a short period of time.

The last time I spoke to my dad was just before the Lord took him home. He had been in and out of hospitals and rehabs, but I got to spend that evening alone with him. We watched television together, and I sometimes just nodded off to sleep beside him, lulled by the hospital monitors. The room was dimly lit, and Christmas music was softly playing from the nurses' station. It was an unusually peaceful moment; I felt calm and comfortable.

Then something (or Someone) within me said, *You need to remind your Dad of how much he means to you.* I fumbled over a few words and then shared, "Dad, I'm so proud of you. You have been a wonderful father to me. You have not only been a good father, but you have showed me something even more valuable and eternal—the love of the heavenly Father. You have shown me how to be a father to my children. I don't think I could have done it without you." I smiled, held his trembling hand, and then with a half-cocked smile, said, "I hope to be like you when I grow up." He just grinned and nodded.

"Well, Dad," I said. "I have to go take care of my family. I need to head home." He nodded but seemed to not want to let go of my hand. "Is there anything I can do for you before I go?"

Almost miraculously, I noticed that the familiar shaking in his hands and legs lessened. His eyes lit up, and I saw that familiar glimmer. Then with great gentleness and care, Dad released my hand and slowly raised his right hand and touched me on the cheek. A lone tear trickled down his face. Dad's voice was steady when he said something I will always treasure. "Son, you already have."

During our last moments together, God set up the most amazing time of my fifty-three years upon the earth—the opportunity to honor my dad and then to hear my dad bless and honor me. There's nothing more that a son or daughter longs to hear. I am blessed by God to have experienced the lifelong love of my father.

# PRAY and Experience Scripture

*He will restore the hearts of the fathers to their children and the hearts of the children to their fathers....* (Malachi 4:6 NASB)

First, ask the Lord to turn your heart toward your father, healing the broken places and restoring the areas of unhealed hurt. Then, using the reflections below, write a tribute to your father, planning just the right occasion to share it and present it to your father. (If your father is no longer living, prepare a tribute anyway. Read it out loud to your spouse or trusted friend.)

*My tribute to* _____, *on the occasion of* _____ _____.

*Dad, as I reflect on my growing-up years, one of my fondest memories was...*

*And I've also been reminded of how we enjoyed...*

*I've come to really appreciate you for how...*

*And how you...*

*As I look to the future, I know I would enjoy it if you and I could...*

*And it would mean a lot to me if we...*

*Dad, I know it is important that I tell you I...*

*And I want you to know how much I love you...*

# LOVE Others in Community

Look for an opportunity to share parts of this tribute with a person who doesn't know Jesus. Talk with them about the healing work that God has done in the relationship with your father. Then tell them about the amazing comfort and care of your heavenly Father.

See *The Forgotten Commandment* by Dennis Rainey for more ideas about how to write a tribute to your father.

# SECTION 3

# PREFACE: HONORING IMPERFECT FATHERS

*Get rid of all bitterness, rage, anger, harsh words, and slander, as well as all types of evil behavior. Instead, be kind to each other, tenderhearted, forgiving one another, just as God through Christ has forgiven you.*

(Ephesians 4:31–32)

## A SPIRIT-EMPOWERED FAITH

lives abundantly "in the present," as His Word brings healing to hurt, anger, guilt, fear, and condemnation, which are hindrances to abundant life. Let these authors encourage your Spirit-empowered faith:

- The Good Dad—Jim Daly
- If You Missed Your Father's Blessing—John Trent and Gary Smalley
- Is It Difficult for Your Children to Honor You?— Roland Warren
- Divorced and Still a Much-Loved Dad—Tammy Daughtry

# 9

# THE GOOD DAD

From *The Good Dad: Becoming the Father You Were Meant to Be*
by Jim Daly

## JESUS, RESET MY FAMILY LEGACY

*Jesus, I want to be a good dad. Empower me to leave behind any hurt I experienced with my own father and live in forgiveness and peace. I want my family's legacy to be filled with hope!*

## PREFACE

"You always hurt the one you love," the old song goes, and it's sadly true. Since our world is filled with imperfect people, our families are filled with imperfect parents and imperfect children. With this much imperfection, it's inevitable that we'll experience hurt. There will be times when you hurt your kids. You will say something harsh or critical. You'll do something that embarrasses them. You'll break a promise or lose your temper. Your kids can hurt you too. They can lie, scream, deceive, and disrespect us. They can get into drugs, alcohol, or in trouble with the law. In all of these situations we can feel hurt and powerless, but God's divine formulas of comfort and forgiveness offer hope.

## Pain's a Part of Relationship

"I can't deal with this. I'm moving back to San Francisco." With those words, my stepfather greeted us after my siblings and I returned home from our mom's funeral—a funeral he didn't attend. They were the last words I ever heard him say.

While my brothers, sisters, and I said our mortal farewells to Mom, my stepdad had started packing. By the time we returned from the funeral, our house had been almost completely emptied —no TV; no green couch; no pictures on the wall. Our clothes had been dumped from dressers and left in piles around the house. A few of our personal belongings dotted the floor—some toys of mine in a box, perhaps a snapshot or two. Anything of real value, anything my stepdad considered valuable, had disappeared, either sold or shipped off. And now he was leaving too. He carried a pair of suitcases to the curb in the twilight. A taxicab was waiting. And just like that, he fled. I never saw him again. He didn't bother to wave good-bye. He never turned around.

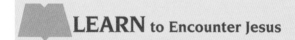 **LEARN** to Encounter Jesus

*Father to the fatherless...this is God.* (Psalm 68:5 NLT)

Jim Daly is an expert on fatherhood—in part because his own "fathers" failed him so badly. His biological dad was an alcoholic. His stepfather deserted him. His foster father accused him of trying to kill him. All of them were out of Jim's life by the time he turned thirteen.

Many of us have had painful experiences with our own fathers. Your story may be similar to Jim's, or you may have had a much less painful relationship with your dad.

Nevertheless, you've experienced some measure of hurt in your relationship with your father. Because your dad was a bad guy? No, because he wasn't perfect.

Reflect for a few moments on some of the ways you have experienced hurt in relationship with your father. Were there times when you felt disappointed, disrespected, discouraged, unaccepted, or rejected? Do you remember feeling afraid, frustrated, scared, or anxious?

*I could have wished for more* _____ (reassurance, comfort, approval, acceptance, forgiveness, patience, etc.) *from my dad. I really needed him to...*

*I often felt* _____ *in my relationship with my dad because...*

Now imagine that Jesus has heard about your hurt. He knows that you've experienced this kind of pain. Just like the story of John 9, Jesus comes to find you (John 9:1–35). He is so moved with compassion for what you've been through that he comes looking for you. And when Jesus meets you, His face is saddened and His eyes are wet with tears. Jesus has been crying for you. Just like the time when Jesus wept for his friend, Mary, Jesus weeps for you. The pain of your heart moves His (John 11:35). The God of all comfort wants to comfort you.

Spend the next few moments telling the Father of compassion about your hurt. Talk to Him about the hurt you've experienced and let Him comfort you. Let Him be a heavenly Father for those things you may have missed from your earthly father. Pour out your heart to Him (Psalm 62:8).

*Heavenly Father, I need some comfort from You about...*

*I need to sense Your compassion because...*

*Speak to me, Lord. I want to listen...*

## To Forgive Is Divine (and Very, Very Hard)

Honesty and forgiveness can heal relationships between fathers and their children. But man, it can be hard to forgive! It's much easier to bury our hurt in a pile of complacency and fool ourselves (or pretend) that we've forgiven. Forgiveness doesn't come easy for us. It's not natural. Revenge is easy, while forgiveness comes primarily through faith, by the strength that comes through Jesus. Anytime you say, "I've forgiven you," even if you say it in your own mind, you should question yourself: Have you really forgiven this person? Or have you simply turned your heart off to the pain? A good test to know your true feelings is to imagine if something happened to the person you've "forgiven." If they died or were seriously injured, what would you feel? Joy? Pain? Indifference? That little test can provide a view into your own heart.

Sometimes what we call forgiveness is really nothing more than a mask, one more tool we use to hide the pain from others and ourselves. Forgiveness is hard.

# PRAY and Experience Scripture

*Get rid of all bitterness, rage, anger, harsh words, and slander, as well as all types of evil behavior.* (Ephesians 4:31 NLT)

Do a brief assessment of your anger, bitterness, and forgiveness. Have you forgiven the people who have hurt you? Consider doing the feelings check that Jim suggested above. *How would I feel if...?* Ask the Holy Spirit to reveal any anger, bitterness, or unforgiveness in your life.

*Holy Spirit, examine my life and show me any anger, bitterness, or unforgiveness that You see in my life. Show me, Lord. I want to live in freedom...*

If the Lord speaks to you about any area of unforgiveness, ask Him to help you get rid of or let go of your anger and hurt. Imagine releasing your hold on your anger and choosing to let it go. Ask the Spirit to empower you to forgive others just like He has forgiven you. Forgiveness is a matter of stewardship. Forgiveness is actually a gift that belongs to the Lord. You have received it, and now He is asking you to give some of His forgiveness to others. Let go of anger. Choose to regift His forgiveness.

*God, I choose to let go of my anger and unforgiveness. Instead, I choose to forgive...*

*Because You have forgiven me, I'm asking You to help me ...*

It's never too late, not as long as we have breath in our bodies. Our relationships may have bent. They may have even broken. But with time and effort and a whole lot of forgiveness, we can mend them. There is hope! There's still a chance to "make a moment" or two. Or twenty. Or two hundred. There's still a chance to reconnect with your father and with your children! There's still a chance to be a good dad.

 ## SHARE with Others in Community

*Mourn with those who mourn.* (Romans 12:15 NIV)

Talk to a trusted prayer partner or small group about the pain you've experienced in relationship with your father. Share vulnerably and allow them to care for you. You might begin with words like these:

*I've asked Jesus to reset my family legacy. One of the steps in that process is gaining freedom from the pain that I experienced in my growing up. Could I talk with you about that? I don't need you to fix anything; I just need you to listen and care.*

 ## LOVE Others in Community

Listen for people around you who don't have a healthy, thriving relationship with their earthly father. Listen to their story. Share appropriate stories of imperfections in the relationship with your dad. Then talk about Jesus and how He wants to know and care about our hurt.

# 10

## IF YOU MISSED YOUR FATHER'S BLESSING

From *The Blessing: Giving the Gift of Unconditional Love and Acceptance*
by John Trent and Gary Smalley

### JESUS, RESET MY FAMILY LEGACY

*Jesus, I want my children, my spouse, my family members, and even my close friends to receive the gift of a blessing. I want to be a conduit of your love, affirmation, and encouragement to others. Remind me often of how you have blessed me, so that I can be a blessing to others.*

### PREFACE

"The blessing" is a gift of affirmation and encouragement that can be life-giving, life-changing experience from father to child. The blessing can be given at a one-time special occasion, but it is also conveyed through consistent, smaller affirmations from parent to child. Helping a child receive and accept the blessing is of tremendous importance. You may have come to realize that you grew up in a home that withheld the blessing—there was no gift of affirmation or encouragement from your father—and this realization has left you feeling hopeless. If so, take heart. You have the wonderful opportunity to overcome the past by extending the blessing to your own children.

## LIFE WITHOUT THE BLESSING

First, let's take a brief look at how missing out on the blessing may affect you. Without the blessing, children can become:

## THE SEEKERS

Seekers are people who are always searching for intimacy but are seldom able to tolerate it. These are the people who feel tremendous fulfillment in the thrill of courtship but may have difficulty sustaining a relationship of any kind, including marriage. Never sure of how acceptance feels, they are never satisfied with wearing it too long. They may even struggle with believing in God's unchanging love for them because of the lack of permanence in the blessing in their early lives.

## THE SHATTERED

These are the people whose lives are deeply troubled over the loss of their parents' love and acceptance. Fear, anxiety, depression, and emotional withdrawal can often be traced to missing out on the family blessing.

## THE SMOTHERERS

These individuals react to missing their parents' blessing by sucking every bit of life and energy from a spouse, child, friend, or others. Their past has left them so empty emotionally that they eventually drain those around them of the desire to help or even listen. When this happens, unfortunately, the smotherers understand only that they are being rejected. Deeply hurt once again, they never realize that they have brought this pain upon themselves. They end up pushing away the very people they need so desperately.

## THE ANGRY

As long as people are angry with each other, they are emotionally chained together. Many adults, for instance, remain tightly linked to their parents because they are still furious over missing the blessing. They have never forgiven or forgotten. As a result, the rattle and chafing of emotional chains distract them from intimacy in other relationships, and the weight of the iron links keeps them from moving forward in life.

## THE DETACHED

Quite a few children who have missed out on the blessing use the old proverb "Once burned, twice shy" as a motto. Having lost the blessing from an important person in their lives once, they spend a lifetime protecting themselves from it ever happening again. Keeping a spouse, children, or a close friend at arm's length, they protect themselves, all right—at the price of inviting loneliness to take up residence in their lives.

## THE DRIVEN

In this category, line up extreme perfectionists, workaholics, notoriously picky house cleaners, and generally demanding people who go after getting their blessing the old-fashioned way: they try to earn it. The thwarted need for affirmation and acceptance keeps these driven people tilting at a windmill named "accomplishment" in an attempt to gain love and acceptance.

## THE DELUDED

Like their driven counterparts, these people throw their time, energy, and material resources into the pursuit of anything they hope will fill that sense of emptiness inside. But instead of focusing on achievement, they look for social status, popularity, attention, and plenty of "toys." These folks are constantly feeling the need to trade in one fake blessing for another.

## THE SEDUCED

Many people who have missed out on their parents' blessing look to fill their relationship needs in all the wrong places. Unmet needs for love and acceptance can tempt a person to sexual immorality, trying to meet legitimate needs in an illegitimate way. Substance abuse and other compulsive behavior can also fall into this category. A drink, a pill, or a behavior is used to cover up the hurt from empty relationships in the past or present, and an addiction can easily result.

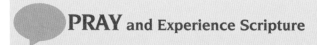

## PRAY and Experience Scripture

*"And you will know the truth, and the truth will set you free."* (John 8:32 NLT)

Take a moment to reflect on the impact of missing elements of your father's blessing above. There are no perfect fathers, so everyone can benefit from receiving more of a specific aspect of their father's blessing. Can you see any connection between missing some of your father's blessing (encouragement, affirmation, or support) and any of the painful outcomes above? Pause and ask the Lord to reveal any needed insights. Ask Him to reveal the truth and empower your freedom.

*Lord, show me the truth about my growing-up years. Are there any areas where I missed some of my father's blessing and I am now living out the impact of that today?*

*I can see how my tendency to* _____ (name one of the struggles above) *may be related to needing more of my father's* _____ (encouragement, support, affirmation, etc.).

## LEARN to Encounter Jesus

*Father to the fatherless, defender of widow —this is God....* (Psalm 68:5 NLT)

Now, hear the Lord's commitment and promise. He *is* the father to the fatherless. Jesus wants to fill in the missing pieces that your earthly father did not fill. Jesus stands ready to give the encouragement, affirmation, or approval that you might have missed. Pause for the next few moments and ask the Lord to speak to you about His desire to be your heavenly Father.

*Lord, please reassure me of Your desire to be my father and give me Your blessing...*

*I especially want to sense Your...*

After this time with Jesus, plan to vulnerably share about your insights and prayer time with a partner or small group.

## THE GIFT OF UNDERSTANDING

I would recommend that anyone who has missed out on his or her family's blessing to understand as much as possible about his or her parents' backgrounds. Following this one bit of advice can help free many people from wondering why they never received the blessing—something I discovered firsthand.

For years I felt pain about the relationship I had with my father. It would often be years between our visits, and he never made contact on his own initiative. His silence trapped a layer of hurt in my life that seemed untouchable... until I met Uncle Max. As I got to know Uncle Max, I took a big step toward really understanding my father—because Uncle Max told me so many stories I had never heard before.

I discovered what life was like at home when he was growing up. I learned much more about his war years and the personal and alcohol-related problems he had suffered as a result of those years. I learned that he had been deserted by his father, just as he had later deserted us.

Learning all these things was like turning on a light in a darkened room. I had often wondered why my father resisted communication with us. Now I saw numerous experiences that had shaped his behavior. I had never understood certain patterns he developed—and then I discovered they actually ran generations deep.

What I learned from Uncle Max was something I hope all children will take into consideration. In the vast majority of cases, parents who do not give the blessing to a son or a daughter have never received it themselves.

If we will stop and take the time to look beyond our parents' actions to their own life story, it will be time well spent. We may even come to realize they need the blessing as badly as we do. And that realization can be the catalyst that frees us to seek the blessing from a more dependable source.

We shouldn't look down and lose hope if we grew up without the blessing. We should look up, instead, to the incredible provision of a blessing that can leave our lives overflowing—the kind of blessing that can even replace a curse with contentment.

 **LOVE** Others in Community

Make plans to share words of blessing with your own kids, spouse, or family. Write out your blessing with three simple steps:

1. Think of one or two things you value and appreciate about your child and jot them down. By choosing just one or two, you're able to really focus your blessing and make your child feel unique. Articulate why you love this about your child and maybe throw in a favorite memory to back it up. Be sure to also include how they specifically bless your life, so your child can understand how their life positively impacts yours.

2. Once you've told your child why he or she is special, pick a challenge your child is facing in the upcoming year, such as a big move or a new job. Acknowledge their fear, but provide encouragement and hope. The purpose of this paragraph is to help your child

"see beyond" the obstacle in their path and remind them of their special future.

3. Write a statement of genuine commitment, sharing how you and the Lord are committed to this child, no matter what. This provides assurance that you'll always love your child through both the good times and bad and reaffirms your commitment to their success.

**Now be sure to create an experience where you share your blessing**. Make it unique to each child, or plan to share the blessing at a special holiday or birthday celebration. Give a gift to memorialize the event. A certificate, special coin, piece of jewelry, or family photo can help a child remember their blessing. Close your time of blessing with lots of hugs and gentle affection.

#  SHARE with Others in Community

Ask God to give you opportunities to share your story of hope with someone else who needs to experience the blessing. Your story might begin with these words:

*I've realized that there were things in my relationship with my father that I missed, but Jesus has filled in the missing pieces by...*

# 11

## IS IT DIFFICULT FOR YOUR CHILDREN TO HONOR YOU?

From *Bad Dads of the Bible: 8 Mistakes Every Good Dad Can Avoid*
by Roland Warren

### PREFACE

The biblical story of Jonathan and his father, Saul, provides us with tremendous examples of what it means to live a life of honor and tragic examples when fathers live without honor. We can't help but notice the contrast between a man who lives for God and the one who lives for himself. Let this contrast motivate you to celebrate the areas where the heavenly Father has made a difference in your life and then change any areas of your life that still need His reset.

### THE RIGHT MAN FOR THE JOB

The biblical account of how Saul rose from obscurity to king gives us some insight into his character as a young man. Specifically, he seemed to have humility and an understanding of the importance of honor. For example, donkey chasing is certainly not the most glamorous of jobs for the most handsome guy in the land. However, he was humbly obedient and did as his father requested. When his servant suggested that they go see Samuel, he listened to a subordinate and was willing to heed his suggestion. In fact, his only concern was that they should have a gift to honor a prophet of Samuel's stature. And when Samuel spoke to Saul for the first time, Saul responded with humility and exclaimed that he was unworthy because his tribe and clan were the least of all. Also, when he met his uncle upon returning home, he certainly could have bragged that he was to be king, yet he said nothing. Finally, Saul held his tongue in the light of praise and ridicule, as the people showed their support by exclaiming, "Long live the king!" followed by naysayers in his own town asking, "How can this fellow save us?" (1 Samuel 10:24, 27).

Saul was blessed with success early in his reign and entrusted with incredible opportunities from the Lord.

## PRAY and Experience Scripture

*Forget none of His benefits.* (Psalm 103:2 NASB)

Reflect on ways God has entrusted you with responsibilities as a husband, dad, and leader. Consider times when God has blessed you:

*No doubt, God has trusted me with the opportunity and responsibility to...*

*I am grateful God has given me opportunity to be involved in...*

It's these reflections that can *humble* us and *protect* us as we remain *grateful* for the privilege of joining Jesus in eternal purposes.

Share your reflections with a prayer partner or small group. Pray together and celebrate the Lord's blessings and opportunities He has provided you. Experience God's Word as you reflect on the benefits He has brought to your life. Remember: gratitude and humility will help guard your heart so that you can be a father worthy of honor.

## KING SAUL'S KEY MISTAKES

Saul began to rule at age thirty and reigned till age seventy-two (1 Samuel 13:1). But it is very clear that Saul began to change over the long course of his reign. He made a number of key mistakes that eventually did great harm to his roles as king and father, moving him into "bad dad" territory.

Saul's first major mistake is recorded in 1 Samuel 13. He was in a battle with the Philistines, and after his son, Jonathan, defeated a garrison of Philistine troops, they responded by mustering a massive force of three thousand chariots, six thousand charioteers, and soldiers "as numerous as the sand on the seashore" (v. 5). Saul only had about three thousand troops, so he and his men headed for the caves to hide. The Bible actually says that these men were "quaking with fear" (v. 7).

However, it's clear from the passage that Saul must have sent word for Samuel to come and give an offering in order to gain God's favor against the massive Philistine force. After waiting seven days, the men began to scatter, so Saul decided to make the offering himself. Saul became fearful when the "market" turned against him. Rather than wait for things to improve (i.e., for God's prophet to arrive), he created a burnt offering that was a fraud.

Samuel arrived just as Saul finished the offering and said, "What have you done?" Saul's response exposed his growing pride, his fear, and a profound lack of trust in God. Samuel didn't mince words, and he told Saul that what he had done was foolish. Saul had broken God's command, and his kingdom would not continue. God would select someone else, a man "after his own heart," to rule the people. In short, Samuel told Saul that the ascribed honor of kingship was being taken from his family line. Saul dishonored Samuel, God's prophet, by usurping his role. He also dishonored God with his lack of trust.

## LEARN to Encounter Jesus

*Your attitude should be the kind that was shown us by Jesus Christ.* (Philippians 2:5 TLB)

In order to avoid the same pitfalls that Saul fell into, ask the Lord how He would like for you to develop more humility and less pride. Stop, pray to the Lord, and listen for His voice.

*Jesus, please show me any attitudes that need to be changed in me. I want my character and Your character to look more and more the same. Speak to me, Lord. I am listening.*

Now complete the following sentences:

- I need to be more *dependent* on the Lord concerning...
  (For example: I need to be more *dependent* on the Lord concerning my important decisions. I tend to quickly decide on a course of action without ever asking God for His direction.)

- I need to be less fearful and more *vulnerable* with _____ about ...
  (For example: I need to be less fearful and more *vulnerable* with my mentor, spouse, or children about my struggles with my temper. I need to share this weakness and ask for prayer for greater self-control. I know God's perfect love can cast out my fear (1 John 4:18).

- I need to be more *trusting* and *approachable*, particularly with _____, especially when...
  (For example: I need to be more *trusting* and *approachable*, particularly with my kids, especially when they are arguing with me about how late they should be able to stay out. I need to trust God more as I listen more closely to them and try to be more open to what they are trying to say.)

Make plans to share your responses with a prayer partner or small group. Pray for each other, asking God to empower each person as they demonstrate more humility, love, and faith.

In contrast to this arrogance and lack of trust, Saul's son Jonathan, though grossly outnumbered, trusted in God, mounted a surprise raid on the Philistine camp, and prevailed. His heroism and courage rallied the Israelite troops, and they were able to defeat the Philistines. What is most interesting about how this occurred is the fact that Jonathan did not tell Saul that he was going to mount this sneak attack. Was it because he was aware fear had led his father to violate God's command and perform the unlawful sacrifice? Or was Jonathan starting to find it difficult to honor a father who had behaved dishonorably? Unfortunately, future events would make Jonathan's dilemma much worse.

As Saul came to terms with the fact that he had lost the kingdom, his behavior became more and more reprehensible. For example, below is a list of a few things that Saul did that, if done by any father, would make it difficult, if not impossible, for a child to honor him:

*Made unwise decisions and treated others harshly* (1 Samuel 14)
*Allowed fear of man to influence him* (1 Samuel 15)
*Allowed jealousy to consume him* (1 Samuel 18:7)
*Lied to his children and used them in dishonorable ways* (1 Samuel 18:21)

As one would imagine, any father who behaved the way that Saul did would make it nearly impossible for his children to honor him. And this certainly was the case regarding Saul and Jonathan. Saul's name was disgraced because of his dishonorable behavior toward God, Samuel, David, and his children. Saul was not able to pass the "family business" on to his offspring. In short, he lost it all. This is a "bad dad" lesson for us all to remember.

#  SHARE with Others in Community

*I will give you thanks in the great assembly; among the throngs I will praise you.* (Psalm 35:18 NIV)

Pause to reflect on your own walk with God. Consider how God has changed you and matured you. How has the heavenly Father helped you to live with honor?

Have you learned to talk with God and trust in Him to answer prayer?

In what ways has Jesus empowered you to teach, train, and instruct your children well?

Has God developed certain godly character traits in you that are clearly evidence of God's power in your life?

Has God strengthened your commitment and empowered you to serve, work, or give effectively to others?

Has the Father revealed specific truths from Scripture that now guide your life and inform your priorities?

Complete these sentences concerning your experiences:

*I praise God for how He has changed me by...*

*I thank the Lord for how He has grown me up by...*

Now plan to share stories of praise for how the Father has enabled you to live as a man of honor. Share with a prayer partner or small group. Rejoice together in how God is changing you to be a dad "worthy of honor"!

# ➤ LOVE Others in Community

Look for people in your life who have missed seeing a dad who lived with honor. Share your stories of hope with words like:

*It must have been so hard for you to miss having a dad who lived honorably. Jesus is my only hope of being a dad who is worthy of honor, because...*

# 12

# DIVORCED AND STILL A MUCH-LOVED DAD

An original article
by Tammy Daughtry

## JESUS, RESET MY FAMILY LEGACY

*Jesus, I want to leave behind guilt and regret so that my life can bring You glory. I want to see the imperfect people in my life with Your vision and Your grace.*

## PREFACE

God often uses pain to accomplish His purposes. He uses brokenness to bring Himself glory! It's often the imperfections of our lives that seem to usher in His pleasure.

Growing up, I always had two homes, one where I lived "full time" and one that I "visited" every other weekend. I never remembered my mom and dad being married or being together as a couple, although they were high school sweethearts and at one time were very much in love.

They grew up in a small farm town in the southwest corner of Colorado, my dad the high school athlete and my mom an athlete and musician. I come from German and Spanish roots, all mixed into what was called a "Heinz 57" blend of cultures. My parents grew up in an area where watermelon and cantaloupe were the hot commodities—one of my grandpas was a produce farmer and the other was a truck driver who delivered produce around the state. I come from great families, great heritage, and great love. Even though my parents divorced, the history of those great families is still a huge part of my personal identity as a woman, a wife, a mother, and now a grandmother.

Looking back, I remember several things about my divorced dad—the *main thing* is that he always showed up! He drove more than an hour to come to my piano recitals, dance recitals, volleyball games, and birthday parties. I never wondered if he would come because he was consistent! He came! He always brought me flowers and gave me a big strong kiss on the cheek as he hugged me with all the pride of his heart.

He remarried when I was three, which means there are some embarrassing photos of me at my father and stepmom's wedding. Those photos reveal a little girl in a yellow dress and white hat "attempting to be" the flower girl for the special occasion. Those family photos continued to grow as God blessed Dad and Josie with a daughter and son: my half brother and half sister. I remember holding my baby brother when I was six years old; he was much more exciting than any baby doll I had been given. And then later, when I was nine I got to have a baby sister in the picture! I'm sure I was quite stingy about holding my little sister when I visited my dad.

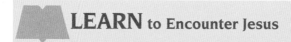

# LEARN to Encounter Jesus

*But God demonstrates his own love toward us, in that while we were yet sinners, Christ died for us.* (Romans 5:8 NASB)

Life brings situations, circumstances, and even people who are not perfect. The good news is that Scripture reminds us that God loves us even while we are imperfect people. Take a few moments to remember some of your "more imperfect moments." Remember the days and times when your behavior, attitude, or relationships were less than stellar. What are your weaknesses? When have you messed up or made choices that you regret?

*Some of my imperfect moments and memories include...*

Now imagine that Jesus has joined you in the living room of your home. He looks into your soul and sees the imperfections of your life. Like home movies on the video screen, Jesus can see every time and every situation where you have been less than perfect. He knows every situation and every relationship when you have messed up or made choices that you regret. And yet, Romans tells us that *even while* Jesus knew every detail of sin and imperfection of your life, He chose to die for you. That's an amazing kind of love!

Jesus demonstrates love toward us even while He knows and sees our imperfections. He declares us worth His love and grace in spite of our behavior. Jesus separates our value to Him from our flaws and imperfections. That's what it means to show honor.

> How does it move your heart to know that in spite of your imperfections, God has declared you worth His honor and worth the gift of His Son?
>
> *God, when I imagine that You know every imperfection of my life and yet still love me, my heart is…*
>
> *When I reflect on the truth that You have given me honor and declared me worth the gift of Your son, I feel…*
>
> How might God want you to demonstrate this same "even-while" kind of love to others?

My dad has always been the life of the party, cracking jokes and talking to every person in the room. He has a strong, extroverted personality, and I am thankful that I took after him—neither of us has ever met a stranger… not in a restaurant, a grocery store, or even a restroom. We talk to people all the time and usually come away from every setting with a newfound friend or at least an enjoyable conversation.

My dad spreads life! He has been a minister for years and takes communion to those who are in the hospital or are shut in and cannot make it to mass. He also takes care of people who need a friend. He has gone to dinner with one of his former employees every other Friday night for at least two decades. She is an older widower who lost her husband in the war, and my dad has become the son she never had; he takes her out for sushi, mows her grass, drives her to the cemetery, takes her shopping, and often takes care of home repairs around her property. He loves her deeply and invests in her with his heart, his time, and his finances.

My dad isn't perfect. He has had some hard years and has certainly made mistakes. His heart has been crushed and hurt deeply by other people, plus he's definitely created his own challenges along the way. Dad carries many regrets and would go back and change many details of his story if he could. But despite the imperfections and the obstacles, my dad loves me. I have never, ever doubted or questioned his deeply felt care for me.

 **PRAY** and **Experience Scripture**

*Forgetting what is behind and straining toward what is ahead....* (Philippians 3:13 NIV)

Reflect on any of the hard years of your life or mistakes you have made. Are there any regrets that you carry or details of your life story that you would like to rewrite?

*I would love to rewrite the part of my life where...*

Now, ask the Holy Spirit to give you the freedom to forget what lies behind you. Ask Him to show you the path of freedom and how to press on to what He desires for your life.

*Jesus, I want to leave behind...*

*Please show me the path to freedom and how to leave my regrets behind...*

*I want to press on to what You desire for my life. Show me what You want for my life.*

My divorced dad may have had a broken marriage, but he did not let me have a broken life. He did everything he could to be sure he participated in my life physically, emotionally, and financially. He shared the burdens of paying for many camps, choirs, plays, trips, and school-related expenses. I'm certain that many of these costs were not "required by law," but he was always present and ready to help. He took me shopping each fall for new school clothes and survived those "choosy teenager moments" with grace and patience. I have the best memories of him getting so tired while I tried on twenty-seven different shirts, pants, and accessories to find "just the perfect one." Knowing what I now know about men and their focused way of shopping, I giggle even more at the long hours of those exhausting trips. My father was probably going crazy inside, but he was with me. He was present and involved.

My dad just keeps showing up! He keeps loving others. My dad keeps giving of himself to care for those around him. My dad keeps showing up for me too. I now live several states away, but he gets on a plane several times a year and comes to see us. I am beyond grateful for his consistency all these years. He never walked away. He never gave up. He never stopped driving and flying to be sure his little girl knew she was loved. Thank you, Dad, for seeing me and investing in me with your heart and your time. Thank you for always believing in me, especially through many detours and surprises along my story. Thank you for always cheering for me and drawing out my best. I love you and I am so proud to call you my dad! I carry your friendly, life-giving attitude with me every single day.

*Dios te bendiga*, Daddy! *Yo te amo*! (God bless you, Daddy! I love you!)

# SHARE with Others in Community

*Freely you have received; freely give.* (Matthew 10:8 NIV)

Ask God to make you a "freely giving" person who meets the same needs in the lives of others that He has met for you. Ask God to continue to bless you abundantly so that you can abundantly give to the family members and friends around you.

Talk to your prayer partner or small group about your plans to give like you have received.

 # LOVE Others in Community

Ask the Lord to reveal one person in your life who needs to receive the "honor" of being loved in spite of their imperfections. Tell them about the source of this great love—Jesus!

*Jesus, show me one person who could benefit from receiving some of Your "even-while" love. Show me how I can be a part of demonstrating that kind of love to them... because of how You have freely given to me.*

# SECTION 4

# PREFACE: THE CALL TO HONOR

*But with God everything is possible.*
(Matthew 19:26)

## A SPIRIT-EMPOWERED FAITH

bears witness to a confident peace and expectant hope in God's lordship in all things. Let these authors encourage your Spirit-empowered faith:

- Fathers Sharing Covenant Love—John K. Vining
- Remembering Dad—Dennis Gallaher
- Biblical Patterns for Spiritual Fathers and Mothers—Billy Wilson
- From Obey to Honor—Brian Doyle

# 13

## FATHERS SHARING COVENANT LOVE
From *Family Ministry Frameworks*
by John K. Vining

### JESUS, RESET MY FAMILY LEGACY
*Jesus, I know that You are the One who created families, and You care about them deeply. Remind me often of how I need to yield to Your desires because You love me and my family so much. Make me a father who sacrifices for my family and prioritizes them with the commitment of covenant.*

### PREFACE
A covenant is a legal term denoting a formal and legally binding declaration of benefits to be given by one party to another. In a biblical covenant, God initiates, confirms, and even fulfills the covenant relationship. From God's perspective, families represent a covenant relationship—one that is marked by death to self, sacrifice, and binding together. How might God want to reframe your perspective of marriage, family, and parenting into what He sees are divinely appointed, covenant relationships?

### COVENANT IS THE CONTEXT FOR FAMILY
Family is valued in the Word of God. The Genesis story is largely an account of not only the instituting of family, but God's dealings

within the first families. The lonely and solitary are placed in families (Psalm 68:6). It is within the family that religious instruction is to take place as a priority (Deuteronomy 6:4–9). The New Testament begins the way the Old Testament ends—with an emphasis on family (Malachi 4:6; Matthew 1; Luke 1:17). Family relationships take on spiritual significance (Colossians 3:18–25; Ephesians 5:21–6:4). Broken families are to be cared for (1 Timothy 5:3, 4; James 1:27).

It is within the context of covenant that such family care is nurtured. Covenant is the bedrock for teachings that impact the family, such as the Great Commandment principle of love (Matthew 22:36–40), the priesthood of all believers (1 Peter 2:5), authority and headship (Ephesians 5:21–32), parental honor (Exodus 20:12), the blessedness of children (Psalm 127:3), spousal love (Song of Solomon), and care for those who are alone (James 1:27).

## PRAY and Experience Scripture

*I will delight in your decrees and not forget your word.* (Psalm 119:16 NLT)

Fathers who are worthy of honor delight in God's Word; they don't forget how His truth has blessed them. Pause for a moment and remember a specific Bible verse that has become especially meaningful to you. Then reflect on how God has made this verse come alive for you. As fathers live in covenant relationship with God and His Word, they provide a firm foundation for living in covenant love with their spouse and children.

Perhaps God used a particular Bible verse (like John 3:16) to draw you out of sin's darkness, remind you of His love, and lead you into a new relationship with Jesus.

Maybe God used a specific Bible promise (like Psalm 23) to lead you out of a challenging experience of your life and remind you that He is your loving Shepherd.

Perhaps God used a specific Bible admonition (like Ephesians 4:31) to challenge you to rid your life of anger, bitterness, or harshness with your family.

Reflect on one of God's Scriptures that has positively impacted you and your family and been a reflection of your covenant relationship with Jesus. Pray these prayers of remembrance to God.

*God, I am grateful to You for using _____ (name Scripture passage) in my life in order to lead me out of _____ and live _____ _____ instead.*

*Lord, I am delighted about Your Word and how it has impacted my life and our family, especially how Your Word reminds me that _____ (principle from Scripture passage). I'm grateful this has made a positive impact on our family, especially how...*

## COVENANT INFORMS FAMILY

The biblical motif of covenant is the pivotal doctrine that informs family. In fact, covenant not only informs us as to the form of family but also its function. Covenant is instructive for the "natural family" and for those in the "household of faith" (Galatians 6:10) and the "household of God" (Ephesians 2:19). That is, covenant extends to all relationships in the home and church. Therefore, "family" includes the married, the unmarried, the separated, the widowed, and the orphaned (1 Corinthians 7; James 1:27). An understanding of this notion is vital because it is in covenant that a man and woman become related to God in marriage, parents and children see their connection to God as family, and the truth of God is experienced in relationship in the church among those of the household of faith. The "Great Commandment Principle" of love (Matthew 22:34–40) is the fundamental expression of covenant. It is summed up in an unequivocal love for God and a self-love equivalent of others. In fact, the telling sign of followers of Jesus is covenant love (1 John 4). To say it another way, without the horizontal experience of covenant relationships, the vertical experience of one's personal relationship with God becomes privatized and undermines the call to community.

## LEARN to Encounter Jesus

*I want your will to be done, not mine.* (Matthew 26:39 NLT)

Our commitment to yield to God is the secret to living in "vertical" covenant with the Lord. Like Jesus, we must be willing to say, "Not what I want, but what You want." Reflect for a few moments on how you are doing at yielding to the Lord. Are you hungry to do what the Lord wants and what He wills for your life?

Take a few moments now to listen to Jesus. He invites you to yield to the Father. Because He knows that the Father's heart is always for our good, His will is perfect, and His plans are best, Jesus invites you to yield. Are you willing to say yes to whatever the Lord asks of you? Even if you do not understand what He is asking, or even if you don't know what He is doing, will you yield to Him? This is a part of what it means to live in covenant relationship with God. When you are ready, pray the following prayer:

*Lord, I yield to You and what You want for me and my family. Show me how You want me to love the important people in my life. I yield to Your will and Your ways. By Your Spirit, empower me to share Your covenant love with my family.*

*In my relationship with my spouse, I yield to You and Your desire for...*

*As I parent my kids, I yield to You in order that...*

After you've prayed to Jesus, consider talking about this encounter with a prayer partner or small group. Tell others how you are yielding to the Lord.

## COVENANT PERSPECTIVE EMPOWERS FAMILY

What is unique about covenant as presented in Scripture is that it is a life-and-death matter. In fact, the notion of contract as a basis for marriage and family living pales when compared to covenant. Features of covenant include:

- The notion of covenant is founded in the Judeo-Christian tradition

- Covenant denotes a special relationship between God and the parties involved
- Covenant was initiated by God
- A covenant was ratified by sacrifice
- Entering into a covenant represented the death of self
- Covenant denotes a binding together

Fundamentally, while a contract represents an agreement between the parties, a covenant mandates a solemn and irrevocable commitment (Genesis 15:12–18; Jeremiah 34:18–19; Matthew 22:36–40; Hebrews 9:16–17).

 **SHARE** with Others in Community

*As each one has received a special gift, employ it in serving one another as good stewards of the manifold grace of God.* (1 Peter 4:10 NASB)

God's grace is like a multifaceted diamond; His grace has different "sides." God's grace includes acceptance, encouragement, comfort, respect, approval, support, and many other beautiful dimensions. These facets are some of the ways that we can serve His grace to others. Only when we die to our will and agenda and yield to His Spirit will we be empowered to share His covenant love in our family.

So how might God want you to initiate additional sharing of His love with members of your family?

Ask the Lord to show you how He wants you to sacrifice your own agenda and instead share some of His grace with your wife, your children, or your family members.

- Who needs more of God's accepting grace—even if their behavior is less than perfect?
- Who might need for you to share some of God's encouragement—believing in them and their abilities?
- Who needs more of God's comfort at this time—words of compassion and care?
- Who needs to receive some of God's approval—affirmation of their value, character, and worth?

Talk with a prayer partner or small group about what the Lord shows you.

 # LOVE Others in Community

Ask the Lord to show you ways that you can be a steward of His grace. Since you have received from Him, ask God to show you how you can share with people who don't yet know Him. Ask yourself the same questions above and reflect on the friends or colleagues who don't yet know Jesus.

# 14

## REMEMBERING DAD
An original article
by Dennis Gallaher

### JESUS, RESET MY FAMILY LEGACY
*Jesus, remind me often of the incredible letter of love that You have given to me through the Bible. Help me to prioritize time to read Your letter daily. Lord, I want my children to have no doubt about my love for them. Help me to prioritize time, energy, and care for them.*

## PREFACE
There's something about a written letter. In a world that's filled with automated text and impersonal responses, a handwritten letter often carries special meaning. What an impact there might be on a generation if every father made it a habit to write letters of love to their children. Imagine the security it would bring to a child if she had a written letter detailing her father's love and reassuring her about his care. Imagine how it would make a son's chest swell with confidence to read a letter signed by his father, "I'm so proud of you" and "I believe in you!" This kind of letter would be treasured for generations to come. This kind of letter could change a family's legacy.

## A Hidden Treasure

The other day I was cleaning out a cabinet that had become unapproachably overstuffed. Out went the magazines that had been treasured for some forgotten cause. Old syllabuses that I had promised to review were promptly removed, and various "to be filed someday" bits and pieces were tossed out with the rest.

As is true of many cleaning projects, I found a hidden treasure that soon had me carefully reminiscing about a man who is really never far from my thoughts—my father, Frank Gallaher.

Dad's been dead a long time, killed in an automobile accident that was totally avoidable. I miss him, to say the least. Anyway, at the back of the cabinet I found a small vinyl notebook with my dad's impressive-looking business card glued to the front: "Frank Gallaher, Vice President, H.B. Engineering, Inc."

I am caught in a flood when I see his name. It's as if he were just there, as if I could call his name or relish time with him. He is gone but never more than a moment's thought away.

I opened the notebook, and another man's name and description was scrawled on a yellow pad. Obviously, my father was flying somewhere and this was his contact... but the handwriting. I had never noticed how much my own resembled his.

Then a flash of a memory: I was a third-grade little boy who continuously made poor grades in penmanship. My teacher was constantly annoyed at the misshapen letters that always seemed to trail off the lines of my Big Chief tablet. The letters that I formed were never a match to those on the blackboard but were a style unknown to everyone but me. No one ever guessed that the style was taken from my hero: my dad.

All my life I've struggled with my sloppy penmanship, and now I look at those nonsensical words on a yellow pad, and it reminds me of the man I've imitated all these years. I actually took that same yellow paper and wrote the words my father had penned so long ago. When I compare my writing with his, it's too close for comfort, if you ask me.

This notebook is all I have of his—a notebook and a handful of his business cards. The final years of my father's life were not good, and bad decisions on top of bad behavior on top of long-practiced habits caught up with him. All that was left of my father's memories was placed on a small table in my home office. "Take whatever you want," my family told me after his death. But when it was time to sort my father's effects, what I wanted was not to be found. How I wished I'd had a letter that would tell me something more of my father's heart.

Each of us can celebrate that our heavenly Father has provided a loving letter for each of us. God *has* written a letter that reveals the Father's heart. Let's take a few moments to reflect on this blessing and the many more we have received from Him.

## PRAY and Experience Scripture

*He who offers a sacrifice of thanksgiving honors me....* (Psalm 50:23 NASB)

Just like a son often emulates the habits, lifestyle, and even penmanship of his earthly father, God's ultimate purpose is for you to emulate Jesus. God's desire is for you to grow into the likeness of Christ so that you can express His life and love to others.

He allows you to receive of God's abundant blessing, sometimes through your earthly father and sometimes through your family, friends, or other followers of Jesus

He enables you to bless others with His love. It is His love that flows through you as you care for your children, your spouse, and your family.

As we give thanks for how we have been blessed, it blesses God and brings Him pleasure.

Reflect on these blessings from the Lord and then honor Him by giving thanks:

*Jesus, as I consider the wonder that You have given me*
_____ *. I am grateful because...*

*And when I remember that my thanksgiving actually blesses and honors You, my heart is filled with...*

## WHAT OUR FATHER THINKS OF US

Isn't it amazing that we have a heavenly Father who *has* written letters to His children? Throughout history, the Father's letters have been written in stone, on leather, or on paper. Our Father's letters have offered comfort and consolation when we can't be physically present with Him.

Miraculously, though, because our Father's letters are *living and active*, they continue to offer to us daily encouragement, invaluable wisdom, and an accurate picture of what our Father thinks of us (Hebrews 4:12 NASB). In the first chapter of Ephesians alone, there are eight statements of how the Father sees His children and what He does for us:

v. 3...    He has blessed us with every spiritual blessing.

v. 4...    He chose us before the foundations of the world.

v. 5...    He chose us long before we chose Him to be His adopted children.

v. 7...    He has redeemed us, bought us from the enemy, and forgiven us.

v. 8...    He lavished His love on us.

v. 9...    He lets us know His secrets.

v. 11...   He has given us an inheritance.

v. 12...   He has placed the royal seal of the Holy Spirit on our lives.

## LEARN to Encounter Jesus

*He will take delight in you with gladness. With his love, he will calm all your fears. He will rejoice over you with joyful songs.* (Zephaniah 3:17 NLT)

Imagine the expression that was on the face of Jesus as you woke up this morning. In your mind's eye, picture His kind, gentle eyes and warm, tender smile. Imagine that as you awoke, God looked down and smiled at you, His precious child. With joy in His heart, He announced, I *am looking forward to spending the day with you!* The heavenly Father, who knows you intimately, cannot wait to care for you, bless you, and share His inheritance with you. The Creator of the universe cannot wait to share the secrets of His kingdom and lavish you with His love (Ephesians 1:3–14).

What does it do to your heart to consider that Jesus is acquainted with all your ways and longs to be intimately involved in your life (Psalm 139:3)? How does your heart respond to the amazing truth that God takes great delight in and rejoices over you?

*When I reflect on my heavenly Father, who cannot wait to show His love for me, I feel...*

*As I consider how my Father rejoices over me and looks forward to spending the day with me, my heart is filled with...*

Say a prayer that communicates your gratitude and wonder.

*Lord Jesus, I feel _____ as I reflect upon Your heart toward me. Thank You for being the kind of God who...*

## THE CONTRAST

Consider the contrast. Written words are an antique commodity compared to the fast track of text messages and all things social media. Where would we be, though, without the written Word of God, signed with the signature of His Spirit on our lives?

Let me suggest two things. First, stop hedging on the importance of God's written Word. Read His Word every day without fail. Nothing can take its place.

Secondly, take time to write to your kids today. It's especially important that fathers and grandfathers write down their thoughts about their children. The thoughts that will endure are the ones that are secured with your handwriting and your signature. The thoughts that will encourage and direct your child are not dependent upon your great wisdom but on the fact that they are in your handwriting and your signature is attached. The letter you author will be a treasure hidden and discovered at the appropriate time. "Like apples of gold in settings of silver is a word spoken in right circumstances" (Proverbs 25:11).

## SHARE with Others in Community

Does God want to change your perspective on your relationship with your children? Does He want to refocus your heart on being more attentive to them or prioritizing of them? God may want to impress you with this truth: of the billions of people on the earth, no one has been called to care for your child's heart more than you! Ask God to show you any changes that might need to be made in terms of your priorities or focus. Ask Him to show you creative ways in which you might give your children a written legacy of your love.

Ask a prayer partner or small group to join you in writing letters of love for your children. Your letters might start with sentences like:

_____, (Call each child by name) *I am so proud to be your Dad because...*

*You are such a gift to our family because...*

*I am amazed by how you...*

*One of the most important things I want you to remember is...*

*I can't wait to see how you...*

*Remember, I love you...*

 **LOVE** Others in Community

Invite other fathers in your neighborhood or community to join you in creating written legacies of love. Explain your commitment to leaving a written record of your love for your children. Invite other fathers to do the same and then plan how you will tell them about the legacy of love from our heavenly Father.

# 15

## BIBLICAL PATTERNS FOR SPIRITUAL FATHERS AND MOTHERS

From *Father Cry: Healing Your Heart and the Hearts of Those You Love*

By Billy Wilson

---

**JESUS, RESET MY FAMILY LEGACY**

*Jesus, refresh my gratitude for the spiritual fathers You've placed in my life. Help me remember all that I have received, and prompt me to give to others in the same ways.*

---

### PREFACE

Scripture gives impactful examples of men and women who have benefited from a spiritual mentor. Let these stories of faith inform your prayers to Jesus.

### SPIRITUAL FATHERS AND MOTHERS

The Bible provides numerous opportunities to observe spiritual parents in action. A nuclear family model of teaching and disciple making is certainly crucial for the formational success of new generations. Biblical models for the nuclear, biological family should be taught and encouraged in Christian communities, since the principal place for disciple making should be in the home. What I primarily want to explore are nonfamilial models in which spiritual parenting and intergenerational mentoring occur. The most trustworthy place to find examples of spiritual parenting is in Scripture.

## MOSES AND JOSHUA

The account of Moses' mentoring relationship with Joshua begins after the exodus from Egypt when Moses selected Joshua to lead the battle with Amalek (Exodus 17). Following this first mention, Joshua's name appears periodically in ways that indicate a close relationship with Moses. Joshua was called Moses' minister and accompanied Moses to Mount Sinai (Exodus 24:13–14). He met Moses on his way down from the mountain (Exodus 32:17). He was called Moses' servant (Numbers 11:28). Joshua served as one of the spies chosen by Moses to go into Canaan and brought back a positive report (Numbers 13, 14). God commanded Moses to position Joshua as his successor, which Moses did (Numbers 27:18, 22). Joshua was lifted up in the eyes of the people and succeeded Moses, leading the Israelites in the conquest of Canaan.

Through these accounts, we witness Joshua fulfilling his destiny and Moses ensuring his legacy. *Success without a successor is actually failure.* Though he did fail at times, Moses avoided failure by having a viable successor in the person of Joshua. He passed the baton to Joshua during his lifetime, ensuring that God's work would continue into a new generation. This is nowhere more evident than in his mentoring of young Joshua to become a great leader. The intergenerational connection between Moses and Joshua was critical to the successful passage of a new generation into the Promised Land. Time spent together, teaching by example, a life of integrity, the influence of blessing, and the power of positive words are all seen in this biblical model.

# **LEARN** to Encounter Jesus

*Give as freely as you have received.* (Matthew 10:8 NLT)

Take a moment to consider the mentors and "spiritual fathers" who have blessed and challenged you. Think about how they shared the love of Christ, taught by example, lived with integrity, or shared positive words with you. Then complete these sentences:

*I have received some of Christ's loving acceptance and support through _____ (name your spiritual father), particularly when he...*

*I was blessed by _____ as he lived a life of integrity and taught me how...*

*I have received some of Christ's loving encouragement through _____, especially when he shared positive words with me. I'm grateful that he said...*

Pause now for two prayerful moments:

First, express your gratitude. *Let all that I am praise the LORD; may I never forget the good things he does for me* (Psalm 103:2 NLT).

*Lord Jesus, my heart is moved with gratitude as I remember how You provided for me in my relationship with _____. I'm especially thankful for...*

Next, listen to Jesus. *"Speak, Lord, your servant is listening"* (1 Samuel 3:9).

*Lord Jesus, because I am so grateful for how I have received from other spiritual fathers, I want to know who I could serve in the same way. Speak, Lord, I'm listening. Show me the person who needs me to give what I have received.*

## NAOMI AND RUTH

The story of Naomi and Ruth is ultimately a story of hope and redemption, but the story began with great struggle. Naomi and Ruth's immigration journey turned horribly wrong when every male family member died in the land of Moab. Naomi buried her family and then turned her heart toward home.

Ruth accompanied Naomi back to Bethlehem, where they lived together in relative poverty until being redeemed by Boaz (Ruth 3–4). Ruth's marriage to Boaz and the child of their union became a blessing to Naomi in her old age (Ruth 4:13–17). In this spiritual mother/daughter model, Ruth made the commitment of loyalty and faithfulness necessary to be a spiritual daughter. Naomi gave wisdom, insight, and discernment to Ruth. As a result, Naomi was blessed in her old age by the fruitfulness of her spiritual daughter.

The story of Ruth reveals the power of loyalty, the impartation of understanding from the aged, and the blessing of a spiritual daughter's fruitfulness. Again, the fulfillment of destiny and legacy occurs in this particular account of spiritual parenting. The story of Ruth and Naomi is an intergenerational testimony of hope in spite of the difficulties of life. God still takes the pain of loss and grief and turns it into joy and blessing, especially when generations love and work together.

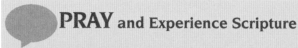

# PRAY and Experience Scripture

*God blesses those who mourn, for they will be comforted.* (Matthew 5:4 NLT)

Recall a time when you were discouraged, saddened, or mistreated, but God brought a mentor or "spiritual father" to comfort and encourage you. How did this person reassure you and show their commitment to you so that you were not alone?

*I remember a time when* _____ *and God brought* _____ *into my life to...*

Celebrate with a prayer partner or small group. Talk about the times when God brought people into your life to encourage, comfort, and reassure you. Acknowledge our great God and how He is at work to now open your eyes and heart to those who need your "spiritual fathering."

## ELIJAH AND ELISHA

The account of Elijah and Elisha is perhaps the most used scriptural example of the spiritual father/son relationship. Elisha is first mentioned in the life of the prophet Elijah on Mount Horeb, where God instructed Elijah to recruit Elisha to take his place (1 Kings 19:16). Elisha committed to follow Elijah (1 Kings 19:21) and became his minister (2 Kings 3:11). Elisha faithfully followed his mentor until Elijah was caught up into the heavens.

Elisha took up Elijah's mantle and entered into prophetic leadership himself (2 Kings 2). This prophetic intergenerational succession forms a model that reveals much regarding spiritual fathers and mothers. We learn that spiritual sons must make a commitment, be willing to submissively serve, continue to be loyal through difficulties, be with the mentor, and be willing to assume responsibility as needed. We also learn that spiritual fathers must clearly hear God's voice in selecting those whom they will adopt as spiritual sons, live in a way that inspires emulation, continue faithful to the call of God upon their lives, leave something for the next generation to take up, and allow their spiritual sons the access needed to succeed.

 **SHARE** with Others in Community

The book of Hebrews says that Jesus "always lives to make intercession" for us (Hebrews 7:25 NASB). His love compels Him to pray for us. He intercedes to the Father for our needs, for our hearts, in our struggles, and in our victories. Imagine Christ kneeling in prayer for you; imagine Jesus speaking your name as He prays to the Father. Imagine that you hear the Savior asking the Father for your victory as a dad and spiritual mentor.

What does it do to your heart to know that Jesus loves you so much that He always prays for you? What impact does it make on your life to know that Jesus prays for your heart to turn first toward Him, then toward your children and toward others who need a spiritual father? Take a moment to tell the Lord about your feelings and then share about this moment with a prayer partner.

*Jesus, when I consider that You are praying for me, my life, and my children, it brings feelings of _____ to my heart.*

## PAUL AND TIMOTHY

The apostle Paul was a spiritual father in the early church. He notes this spiritual fatherhood with the Corinthian believers: "For though ye have ten thousand instructors in Christ, yet have ye not many fathers: for in Christ Jesus I have begotten you through the gospel" (1 Corinthians 4:15 KJV). Although he was a spiritual father for many early Christian communities, Paul's personal spiritual fathering role is seen most clearly in his relationship with Timothy. Paul, heeding the advice of the brethren, selected Timothy to travel with his ministry team (Acts 16:2). Timothy came from a family in which his mother was a believer and his father was not (Acts 16:1). Timothy had a strong Christian heritage from his mother, Eunice, and his grandmother, Lois (2 Timothy 1:5). Yet Timothy needed a spiritual father in order to reach his full potential in Christ. Paul called Timothy his son (1 Timothy 1:2, 18; 2 Timothy 1:2; 2:1) in the faith.

The model of Paul and Timothy is one of the clearest in Scripture for defining the roles of spiritual parents and spiritual children. The writings recorded in 1 and 2 Timothy are instructions of a spiritual father to his spiritual son, and Timothy's faithful discharge of service is a prime example of the commitment needed by spiritual sons and daughters. Timothy served Paul in the good times and the bad (Acts 16). Timothy could be trusted (Philippians 2:19–20). Timothy was empowered by Paul to do the work of ministry (1 Timothy) and was corrected by Paul in the midst of that work (2 Timothy). At the end of his journey, Paul's spiritual son, Timothy, ministered to the aged apostle (2 Timothy 4:9–21).

Christianity has survived throughout history because one generation has passed the faith on to another. Sometimes we have been more successful at this than at other times. The twenty-first century has brought us to a new season of spiritual transition, one in which the younger generation must not move too fast and the older generation must push themselves to get the baton passed. We are intersecting together in God's passing zone. If we follow the pattern of Scripture, spiritual fathers and mothers will not fail to impart to their spiritual sons and daughters the passion, purpose, and purity needed to finish the race. Together we can win. Apart we will be disqualified.

 **LOVE Others in Community**

Make a plan to share about one of your spiritual mentors. Plan to share this aspect of your faith with someone who doesn't yet know Jesus.

*I'm so grateful for the impact of _____ on my life. I'm grateful because he/she has a life that's been reset by Jesus. I can see the difference Jesus has made in his/her life because...*

*I'm thankful that I get to do life with someone who...*

# 16

## FROM OBEY TO HONOR
An original article
by Brian Doyle

> **JESUS, I WANT TO RESET MY FAMILY LEGACY**
> *Help me honor my father, spiritual mentors, and other authorities You have placed in my world. I want to listen to Your voice as You show me any childish things that need to be put away.*

### PREFACE
Just as there is a God-designed transition from childhood to adulthood, there is a God-designed transition for many of us from obeying our father to truly honoring him. Resetting a family legacy will require both of these transitions.

### THE COMMAND TO OBEY
The family is the place where children are taught directly and indirectly from the very beginning the importance of obeying authority. This is always with the best interests of the child in mind. An engaged father who loves and cares for his child will both teach and train his child to obey authority because he knows that is what's best for the child.

Most men that I know talk about "first-time obedience." This is simply when a father gives a clear instruction and the child immediately responds by obeying the instruction. It is also prudent that children are taught to verbally communicate a word of affirmation such as "Yes, Dad" when obeying the instruction. This confirms that the instruction is heard and is also an early step in preparing the child to make the transition from obedience to honor. The heart attitude behind obeying the instruction is part of a father's training. Following instructions is not complete obedience. A child must be taught to respect and trust authority.

## THE IMPORTANCE OF FIRST-TIME OBEDIENCE

When our children were young, we lived on a somewhat busy street. Our children were taught that when they heard Dad or Mom or an older sibling communicate the command, "Stop!" they were to immediately stop. There was no option to consider if stopping was their heart's desire or if stopping fit into their predetermined goals and objectives. When they heard that word, they were to immediately obey. The fact that the child's safety was involved made this a relatively easy command for children to learn to obey.

Other commands are not directly connected to a child's safety and can be more challenging to create a pattern of first-time obedience. In our home, when it was time to prepare for bedtime, the instructions given would not have the same urgency as when we were trying to keep the kids away from the busy road. The tone of voice was different, but it was still a command with an expectation of obedience and affirmation. As a parent, I needed to be able to offer grace and be flexible, but it was still my responsibility to expect first-time obedience. A father who consistently expects obedience is much easier for a child to follow than a father who gives mixed messages by his failure to require consistent obedience. Our children learned to obey without the need to have urgency in our voice.

A child who has learned to properly obey his father and mother in the context of his family is most prepared for obeying the authorities he will meet outside of the home. At a relatively young age, children are often under the supervision and authority of teachers and coaches and other adults. The pattern of obeying their father and mother is put to the test with these new relationships. The fruit of family life is often quickly seen by the respect or lack of respect that a child shows to teachers and coaches and other adults. This is still a time of training, and fathers must stay engaged and help teach their children to execute first-time obedience. In addition, the child must obey with respect for this new authority and learn to deal with poor attitudes. Coming soon in the life of every child is the need to obey and respect public servants such as police officers and employers and different supervisors at work.

 **PRAY** and Experience Scripture

*Let the message about Christ, in all its richness, fill your lives.* (Colossians 3:16 NLT)

Take the next few moments and allow the Lord to remind you of a wake-up call you received from the Lord—a time when you realized obedience to your earthly authorities was important just as obedience to our heavenly Father is important. When did this specific part of Christ's message fill your life and bring blessing?

> Lord, help me remember some of the times when my obedience to authorities brought blessing and richness to my life.

Consider sharing this response with a prayer partner or small group.

*I remember a time when the Lord got my attention by...*

*I learned how important it is to obey the authorities in my life when...*

## CHILD TO ADULT AND OBEDIENCE TO HONOR

The twenty-first century Western culture sends mixed signals on when a child becomes an adult. Consequently, there are mixed messages on when a child moves from operating under the direct authority of the parent to a place where honor replaces obedience. This confusion impacts both the child and the parent. What are some of the sources of this confusion? Here are several:

- Voting age is 18
- License to drive is 16
- Right to purchase alcohol is 21
- Adult price at amusement park is 12
- Employment age can begin at 14

There is simply no clear marker in the current culture for parents and children on when a child becomes an adult. This lack of a clear marker brings confusion to the transition from obedience to honor. This does not mean that the transition cannot be smooth, but it does mean that it will likely look different from family to family.

## A Rite of Passage

One marker of the Jewish faith community that gives clarity to when a child becomes an adult is the bar mitzvah for boys or bat mitzvah for girls. This includes a traditional ceremony at age thirteen, and the result is that the young adult is now accountable for his or her own actions and may fully participate in the life of the faith community. This marker brings clarity to the relationship between the child and the parent and is done in the context of community so that it is not just a family decision.

My oldest son and I invested the better part of a week to gather with other Christian fathers and sons to mark the transition from childhood to adult. We shared some adventure together in the mountains and some teaching together on biblical manhood. We enjoyed the friendships and community of men in the same season of life and concluded our time with a ceremonial rite of passage where each dad called his son out of childhood and into the community of men. There was exhortation and there was celebration. Both contributed to clarity of the marker.

The apostle Paul also had a relationship marker of his own. He shared it with us in 1 Corinthians 13:11: "When I was a child, I spoke and thought and reasoned as a child. But when I grew up, I put away childish things" (NLT).

## LEARN to Encounter Jesus

*Yes, ask me for anything in my name, and I will do it!* (John 14:14 NLT)

Spend the next few moments asking Jesus to reveal any areas of your life where you might still speak, think, or reason as a child or display childish actions. Ask the Lord to show you any childish ways that need to be put away.

*Lord Jesus, show me any ways that I need to change from childishness to maturity. Speak, Lord, I am listening.*

Now, let this day be the marker of when God brings about change. Thank Jesus in advance.

*Jesus, I thank You in advance for changing me. I know You want this change for me and You promised to do it. So I am looking forward to growing in...*

### CHOOSING TO HONOR

Although I did not have a rite of passage that transitioned me from childhood to adulthood, I did leave home and go away to college. At the age of seventeen, this was my marker. Having a job and driving a car were not nearly as significant as leaving home. Moving out of my parents' house moved me into adulthood. I had moved from obeying my father to honoring him. I chose to keep my father and mother engaged in my life by returning their calls and occasionally even calling them. I shared my challenges and my successes. I visited home regularly and asked for input on decisions when it was appropriate. My father and mother were willing and even eager for involvement but worked hard to respect this new season of life.

It seems like families today are having a more difficult time letting go and allowing children to transition into adulthood. Fathers must take the lead in this effort by stepping back from daily involvement and yet still communicating interest and concern. This is the opportunity to show confidence in a son or daughter's ability to handle new responsibilities. This is the time to set the stage for the move from obedience to honor. This is the faith step: trusting God that your many years of investment will not be in vain. It will take intentionality and solid communication between parents and children to transition from obedience to honor, but this transition is critical for a meaningful family legacy.

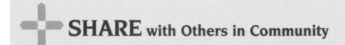

# SHARE with Others in Community

*I thank my God in all my remembrance of you, always offering prayer with joy....* (Philippians 1:3–4 NASB)

Reflect on a time when your father (or a spiritual father) demonstrated trust in you. When did this person trust that you could make your own decisions, discern a solution, or make a right choice? Perhaps a father, grandparent, or other family member demonstrated confidence in you or related to you with an extra measure of respect. Was there a challenging time or crisis in your life when a mentor entrusted you with more responsibility or demonstrated by their actions that they believed you "could handle it"? Reflect on these memories here:

 I *remember when* (name)_____ *trusted in me about...*

*I'm so grateful when I remember this because...*

Now, plan to share these remembrances with a prayer partner or small group. As God stirs your heart with gratitude, remember this: it's gratitude for how others have trusted you that can prompt you to gratefully put trust in others (Matthew 10:8).

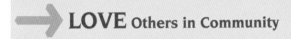 # LOVE Others in Community

Make a plan for how you will tell others about the blessing that has come to your life as you have learned to honor your parents, not just obey them (Ephesians 6:2–3). Talk about how God's truth works! Your words might begin with these:

*I am amazed at how God's promise works. When we honor our parents, life goes well for us. I've seen this in my life...*

# SECTION 5

# PREFACE: BEING A FATHER WORTHY OF HONOR

*He will restore the hearts of the fathers to their children and the hearts of the children to their fathers….*
(Malachi 4:6 NASB)

## A SPIRIT-EMPOWERED FAITH

yields to the Spirit's protective cautions and transforming power to bring life change. Let these authors encourage your Spirit-empowered faith:

- Are You Worthy of Honor?—Dennis Rainey
- Loving Your Children's Mother—Carey Casey
- Sexual Integrity: Finding Your Path—Tony Dungy
- The Culture-Wise Family—Ted Baehr and Pat Boone

# 17

# ARE YOU WORTHY OF HONOR?

From *The Forgotten Commandment*

by Dennis Rainey

## JESUS, RESET MY FAMILY LEGACY

*Jesus, help me to prioritize involvement with my kids and be "all in" when it comes to their interests and activities. Lord, make me sensitive to times when my child needs my affection and emotional support. Help me take initiative to say "I love you" and give lots of reminders of how much they mean to me.*

### PREFACE

"Honor your father and mother. Then you will live a long, full life in the land the LORD your God is giving you" (Exodus 20:12 NLT). This commandment is easy for some, challenging-but-possible for others. Yet it stands as God's will for children of every age and all circumstances. So much is lost when we neglect this command—the emotional connection of expressed love, the bonding of generations, the healing of past pain, and the real possibility of family reconciliation.

## WORTHY OF HONOR

*A good character is the best tombstone. Those who loved you and were helped by you will remember you. So carve your name on hearts and not on marble.* (C. H. Spurgeon)

Years ago I had an unusual speaking opportunity. First I addressed a group of teenagers, exhorting them to heed the command of Ephesians 6:1–3, which instructs children to *obey and honor* their parents. Then I had the opportunity to speak about the same passage to the parents of those teens. But the moment I'll never forget from that gathering was when Dr. Henry Brandt, a psychiatrist from West Palm Beach, Florida, posed this question to those parents: "Are you worthy of honor?"

I remember the room was strangely quiet. Most had never considered the question. And many had to answer Brandt with a sheepish, "No... I'm really not worthy."

How can you make it as easy as possible for your children to honor you?

It's been fascinating to read through the special tributes that adult children have written for their parents over the years. The memories in these tributes form a mosaic of what a family ought to be. Over and over, the children who wrote tributes considered three things important:

- Their parent's involvement
- Their parent's emotional support
- Their parent's character

Let's consider how we can become a parent worthy of honor by building these qualities into our lives.

PRINCIPLE #1: YOUR CHILDREN WILL REMEMBER YOUR INVOLVEMENT.

Your children need more than your time; they need your attention. They flourish when you focus on them.

This means more than just showing up at soccer games. Children need your heart knitted to theirs as they make choices and hammer out their character. They need you to know what's going on in their lives. They need you to help them think about the clothing they wear, the type of person they date, and the peer pressure they face.

In order to be a parent worthy of honor, you can't just *be* there, you have to be *all* there.

That sounds simple, but it's easy to fill your hours away from work with television shows, the Internet, hobbies, finances, books, shopping, and housework. If you were able to add up how much time you actually spend focusing on your children each week, you might be shocked to discover that your total would be measured in minutes, not hours.

Being all there does not mean you do it perfectly every time, but it does mean that you are keeping the lines of communication firmly open and intact.

## LEARN to Encounter Jesus

*Thanks be to God for His indescribable gift.* (2 Corinthians 9:15 NIV)

Take a moment and reflect on Jesus. His very nature is to be with and give first to us. He is determined to be "all there" for us despite our selfishness and our prideful self-reliance. He gives first in the face of our competition, comparisons, and division. Jesus was all there even in the midst of our sin (Romans 5:8).

What do you feel as you consider Jesus' response to you? How is your heart stirred by the knowledge of how He longs to be with you? How are you affected as you sense that Jesus is "all there" for you, wanting to love you and give to you?

Express your gratitude for the heart of Jesus that gives first.

*Jesus, I am grateful for Your heart of love, a love that gives first especially as You…*

*I am overwhelmed by feelings of…*

*I want the love that I have received from You to empower my love for my children.*

## PRINCIPLE #2: YOUR CHILDREN WILL REMEMBER YOUR EMOTIONAL SUPPORT.

I will never forget a counseling appointment many years ago. A mom sat in my office and told the story of her eleven-year-old son's relationship with his dad. The father, a hard-driving and successful businessman, constantly criticized the boy.

"You dummy, you left the door open."

"Look at these grades! That's pitiful!"

"You struck out at the game! I can't believe you did that!"

By my estimate that boy is in his late forties now. And I'll bet he still hears an inner recording repeatedly playing. *You're a failure! You can't do it! Why try?*

Some of you know how painful it feels to hear that inner recording day after day. Is this the type of recording you want for your children?

Reading through tributes, I've also observed how adults do remember the positive emotional support they received from their parents.

> *I can't remember a time that you didn't accept me. I was always okay. My performance was okay, too, as long as I tried my hardest. You encouraged me to develop the talents God had given me. You told me about how it thrilled you to feel me stir within you before I was even born whenever music was being played at church. You were always there to encourage me in my lessons and shine with pride at my success.*

How often do you tell your children you love them or forgive them? Your kids should hear these words so often that they have no idea how often you've said them.

Another way to give your children emotional support is by utilizing the power of the printed word. Letters and notes are tangible reminders to your children that you love and care for them. Young children, especially, will treasure your handwritten notes of affection.

Emotional support is also felt when we physically touch our children. Hugs, tight embraces, and kisses are all the steady practice of a parent who wishes to be worthy of honor.

I've found that if dads give physical and emotional affection when their children are young, it won't be nearly as difficult when they become teens. It's difficult sometimes to hug teenagers, because they act like they don't need it. But that's just a facade.

I'll never forget Barbara hugging our son Benjamin after a rough day at his junior high. She let go; he didn't. He was admitting, nonverbally, *I may be nearly as tall as you, and I may look grown up, and I may act like I don't need affection, but I do!*

By filling and refilling our child's emotional tank, you and I become worthy of honor.

 **PRAY and Experience Scripture**

*Now that you have purified yourselves by obeying the truth… love one another deeply, from the heart.* (1 Peter 1:22 NIV)

How might you better express Christ's love to your children?

Make plans to show love to your child in one of these four ways. You might write a note or share these words in person:

**Appreciation** (for things they do)

_____ (name), *I appreciate all that you do to make our family great. I've especially noticed how you…*

*Thank you for the way you help with…*

**Encouragement** (in the midst of a struggle)

_____ , *I know that it's been hard to…but I know you can…*

*I want to encourage you in…because I believe in you and know that you…*

**Celebration** (about a positive event in their life)

_____, I am so happy that you...It makes me smile to know that...I'm excited that you..._

**Comfort** (about a painful event/issue in their life)

_____, I'm so sorry that you're going through this... I feel a lot of compassion for you because..._

Pause now to ask Jesus to empower you to express love to your children deeply and frequently.

PRINCIPLE #3: YOUR CHILDREN WILL REMEMBER YOUR CHARACTER.

As a parent, you have the incredible responsibility of shaping the moral conscience of the next generation. Even though your children will grow up to make their own choices, the character qualities you model and teach will help mold them and give them direction. In fact, I've noticed that many children, after passing through years of rebellion against their parents, settle into adult-hood by adopting many of the same character qualities that they once railed against.

Once again, I found these character qualities highlighted often in the tributes I've read:

_You taught me through example to honor and respect my elders, to establish a strong work ethic, and to complete a task with excellence. You are a man of your word._

What character qualities do you want to pass on to your children? What do you believe in? What are your core values?

The Roman philosopher Seneca said, "You must know for which harbor you are headed if you are to catch the right wind to take you there." If you've determined what your core values are, then you can find creative ways to teach and model them to your children.

## A Special Challenge to Dads

Over the last few decades, too many fathers have pulled back from leadership in their families. To a large degree, we who call ourselves "dads" are responsible for this paralysis of character in our homes. Too many of us are passively disengaged, consumed with our careers, preoccupied with our toys and hobbies. We're too disengaged to get involved with our kids' lives.

Real men with real character act; they take responsibility head-on. They may not do it perfectly, but they tackle issues courageously. They are men worthy of honor. They step up when faced with tough challenges.

Men, we need to hear and heed Paul's words to the church at Corinth: "Be watchful, stand firm in the faith, act like men, be strong. Let all that you do be done in love" (1 Corinthians 16:13–14).

We've got to encourage one another to be involved and not abandon our kids to the culture. We've got to do it because God is going to hold us responsible for how we protect our families.

God will help you be worthy of honor and involved in your child's life. Just ask Him to reconnect your heart to your children's.

**SHARE** with Others in Community

*Use your freedom to serve one another in love.* (Galatians 5:13)

Talk about the insights you have as a result of the prayer moments above. Discuss these with a prayer partner or small group. Practice sharing words of appreciation, encouragement, celebration, and comfort with one another. Let these moments be times where you practice connecting emotionally with one another so that you are better equipped to connect with your children.

 **LOVE** Others in Community

*This is the confidence we have in approaching God: that if we ask anything according to His will, He hears us. And if we know that He hears us—whatever we ask—we know that we have what we asked of Him.* (1 John 5:14–15 NIV)

After you have effectively prioritized your own kids and grandkids, ask Jesus to show you a person within your sphere of influence who is "fatherless." Ask God to show you how you can be a spiritual father to this person. Discuss this insight with a prayer partner or small group and then pray together.

*Heavenly Father, do in my heart and life whatever You need to do for me to impart my life and the gospel. Help me to accept any role You have for me as a "spiritual father." Thank You for hearing my prayer and accomplishing Your will in my life.*

# 18

## LOVING YOUR CHILDREN'S MOTHER

From *Championship Fathering*
by Carey Casey

> ### JESUS, RESET MY FAMILY LEGACY
> *Jesus, help me to remember that one of the best ways to be a great father to my kids is to be a great lover of their mom. Jesus, empower me to love her well.*

### PREFACE

Loving our kids starts long before they're born. If we want to truly love them, we start by loving their mother. It's obvious that a lot of people are missing this, but a protected-by-marriage love ought to be in place when children are conceived. This same shelter of love remains the ideal environment in which to raise kids to maturity.

Even though many people are trying to do this parenting thing in every other way possible, it's not hard to see that God's system was designed for a man and woman to make a child and then raise that child. If men can't even *become* fathers without a woman's help, it makes sense to recognize that effective fathering will also involve a woman.

## A Note to Divorced and Never-Married Dads

If you're reading this as a dad who's divorced or never married, you may wonder how this applies to you. It's not my purpose to assign blame or to offer a fix for your situation. But I can say that you, too, need to account for your children's mother in your efforts to be an effective father.

I believe that even when a marriage has been destroyed by the tragedy of divorce, a father must treat the mother of his children with a respect that shelters those children. This is also true of dads who have fathered children but have not married the mother.

## A Father's Challenge

"Husbands, love your wives." Simple, right? We asked them to marry us because we loved them. We vowed in the wedding ceremony that we would love them, and it's hard to come up with a believable explanation that lets us off the hook for our promises. If I'm a husband, one of my number-one jobs is to love my wife.

So how do we approach this challenge? By figuring out what kind of chocolate she likes? By remembering her favorite flowers? By getting an administrative assistant or computer to remind us when the anniversary is coming up?

For many of us, loving our wives seems like a problem to be solved, a mystery to be unraveled. This is where we sometimes get off track; loving our wives is not a puzzle, it's a journey to discover and maintain for a lifetime.

Our research often points to the overwhelming need for a father to love and respect the mother of his children. How do you start? If you're married and haven't done this lately, listen up.

Today, I want you to go home and walk in and plant a big kiss on your bride's lips, right in front of your kids.

They'll probably react. Expect to hear, "Oooh, Dad! What are you doing? I can't look!"

They may be a little embarrassed, but they need to see this passion and deep love in your marriage. They might not ask, but they do wonder if you love their mom. In fact, the evidence of an unbreakable and healthy bond between you and your wife is actually a wall of security around your children.

When our oldest son, Marcellus, was thirteen and I told him his mother was pregnant, he leaned against the window and shook his head. "Oooh, gross, Dad. You mean y'all still do that?" At the time we had three kids, so he must have thought we'd "had fun" just three times.

"Homey," I said, "let me school you up. God made sex. Hugh Hefner didn't make sex. Larry Flynt didn't make sex. That lying stuff on the computer, that billion-dollar industry called pornography, is a lie. That's counterfeit. God made sex! It's not bad! It's one of the greatest joys God made to bring husband and wife together. It's in His plan for pleasure as well as procreation. I'm shooting you straight, Son. You're gonna have a brother or sister."

Somehow both of us survived that conversation.

It's up to us to communicate to our children what marriage and romantic love are all about. We do it best by example—showing love to our brides and serving them. We also teach our kids by talking about it when opportunities come up. Let's make sure they get a clear picture of marriage from God's perspective.

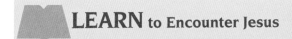

# LEARN to Encounter Jesus

*Have this attitude in yourselves which was also in Christ Jesus.* (Philippians 2:5 NASB)

God may want to impress you with this truth: of the seven billion people on the face of this planet, no one has been called to love your spouse more than you! So how will you better express your love to your wife?

Might God want to change your attitude in your relationship with your spouse? Could Jesus want to reset the way you see your partner—not as a problem to be fixed or tolerated, but a gift to be cherished?

Ask God to show you any changes that might need to be made.

*Jesus, show me any attitudes that are true of Jesus that need to be true of me, especially in relationship with my spouse. I want our marriage to be an example and blessing to our children. Show me how I can build this wall of security even stronger for our kids. Speak, Lord, I am listening.*

## SAY "I LOVE YOU"

We can train ourselves to say "I love you" to our wives, but we shouldn't say those words just because they're a requirement. Instead, reflect on some of the many reasons you have for loving your wife and try this: turn to your wife and say, "I've got something very important I have to tell you—I love you." The fact that you've placed some emphasis on this may provoke an unusually positive response.

Also, be prepared to answer the "Why?" question when you tell your wife you love her. Or answer the question at times without being asked. "Do you want to know why I love you?"

You'll have her undivided attention. She won't be able to wait to hear what you say next, so make it good! Give the next three sentences you say some careful thought. Make them your own. Here are a few ideas to help you through that process.

*Why are you content in a love relationship with this woman?*
Because she challenges you to be a better man?
Because she's an amazing mother to your children?
Because of the way she understands and repeatedly forgives you?
Because of what she's taught you about love?

Be prepared to give at least three brief statements to back up your declaration of love.

When you communicate love to your wife, focus on how she feels loved rather than your own confusion and difficulty. Perhaps words don't really "say" love to her. To find that out, become an attentive student of your woman. It doesn't hurt to ask, "What words or actions communicate love to you most clearly, babe?" Or even, "Would you tell me about some times in your life when you really felt loved?" You may be surprised at how specific she is.

Sometimes we miss the mark in expressing love, and it hurts to find that out. We can bring chocolates home every week only to discover that she feels fat rather than loved. We might buy flowers then hear that she'd rather we volunteered to do the dishes. The road to learning is paved with little failures like these, but we have to get over them.

Once we find out what makes our woman feel loved and secure, we've got to get busy making sure she gets plenty of it! She's probably not going to give you a list, though. Even if she does, do your best not to let her know you're working from it.

If she says, "When you take care of something that's broken around the house or carry out the garbage without my asking, that makes me feel loved," don't make your response obvious. When she isn't looking, do the things she mentions. Don't wear a "Mr. Fix-it" T-shirt and put a neon sign on your forehead that flashes, "Watch me take out this trash, baby!"

Your children will be watching most of this. They'll be "catching" it in ways they may not even be aware of. They won't think, *I'll have to remember this for later.* But someday they'll do something for their spouse and it will dawn on them: *This is just what Dad used to do for Mom.*

Watching the way you treat their mother will create an invisible but indelible record in their hearts and minds.

## PRAY and Experience Scripture

*Let no unwholesome word proceed from your mouth, but only such a word as is good for edification according to the need of the moment, so that it will give grace to those who hear.* (Ephesians 4:29 NASB)

The words that come out of your mouth will also leave an indelible imprint on your children. So pause for a few moments and consider the words you might say about your spouse (in front of your kids). This is how to meet your wife's relational need for approval. *Approval* is "building up and affirming another person, affirming both the fact of and importance of a relationship."

Take a moment to think about your wife. What specific character qualities do you admire in her? What positive character traits have you noticed, and when have these traits been demonstrated?

Plan how you will finish this sentence about your wife:

I *have been blessed by your* _____ . *And I saw this quality in you when...*

(For example: I *have been blessed by your enthusiasm.* I *saw this quality in you when we worked together in children's church. You were always excited to see the kids and thrilled by the chance to teach them about God's Word.*)

(For example: I *have been blessed by your patience. And* I *saw this quality when you shared about your difficult situation at work.* I *have been impressed by your acceptance of all that has happened and your willingness to wait on the Lord.*)

Here is a list of other character qualities:

| | | |
|---|---|---|
| Boldness | Endurance | Initiative |
| Compassion | Fairness | Loyalty |
| Contentment | Faith | Responsibility |
| Creativity | Flexibility | Sensitivity |
| Determination | Generosity | Sincerity |
| Diligence | Gentleness | Understanding |
| Discernment | Gratefulness | Wisdom |

Plan a time to share your words of approval with your wife both privately and publicly. Saying these words in the presence of your children will also provide them with great security, and you'll be a tremendous role model in your home!

## TOUGH LOVE

Love between a husband and wife is more than cuddling by a fireplace or talking about what makes you feel good. Sometimes it's the opposite of staying warm and toasty. Sometimes love requires a toughness that complements the tenderness.

At certain times love means doing things you don't feel like doing. Love means doing the hard things. Love might mean hiking for groceries on a cold morning, washing the dishes or doing mountains of laundry, getting up at 3 a.m. to feed the new baby, or bringing the shoes that your child has forgotten...again!

Sometimes love feels like drudgery because it involves the daily grind! It's more about perseverance than it is about songs and sighs. As numerous authors have correctly pointed out, love is a choice we keep making. It isn't something we do because it makes us feel good or because we think we're going to be rewarded. Love focuses entirely on the other person.

Now, don't get me wrong. Romance is a good thing. It was designed by God to bring husbands and wives closer. Flowers, date nights, pet names, and sex are a big part of marriage. But they're not everything.

If your bride is truly a high priority, the way you value her should be seen in the way you serve her—the hard work, the sacrifices, the inconveniences. Think of her first, tune in to her needs, and follow through.

#  SHARE with Others in Community

*I pray that the eyes of your heart may be enlightened, so that you will know what is the hope of His calling, what are the riches of the glory of His inheritance in the saints.* (Ephesians 1:18 NASB)

Pray with another Jesus follower, asking the Holy Spirit to fix your heart on the words, "in the saints." Many of God's glorious riches are already in your wife (one of His saints)! And one of the ways you can serve your wife is to vulnerably express your needs. If you need acceptance in the midst of self-doubt, God might want to provide some acceptance through the riches that are in your bride. If you need encouragement, care, or affirmation when you grow weary in well-doing, God may provide through her love. It is still His acceptance, His encouragement, and His care, but God shares them with you through your wife.

Pause and pray together, celebrating with a glad heart, giving thanks for your wife, and expressing to the Lord your desire to better love and serve her.

After you've prayed with a prayer partner, consider sharing these vulnerable words with your wife:

*I've realized that I need more of your* _____ (acceptance, reassurance, encouragement, care, affirmation, etc.) *regarding...And so I think it would mean a lot to me if...*

**LOVE** Others in Community

Ask Jesus to reveal one other father who could benefit from your encouragement and challenge in loving his wife well. Make plans to share what God wants to change in you and encourage your friend to consider the same.

*I'm trying to be the best dad I can be. And I've realized that one of the most important things I can do to be a great father is to love my wife well. Here's what God has been showing me...*

# SEXUAL INTEGRITY: FINDING YOUR PATH
From *Uncommon Man*
by Tony Dungy

## JESUS, RESET MY FAMILY LEGACY
*Jesus, I want to please You—especially in the area of sexual integrity. Empower me to stand firm in the convictions that You have given for my life. Surround me with other men who will encourage me and challenge me to live uprightly.*

## PREFACE
As awkward as it is, we need to be more up-front about sex and its effect on our lives as men. Any sex outside of marriage—during or before—is wrong. Most of us would agree that infidelity while you're married is wrong, but we wouldn't get a consensus on sex before marriage. You may not agree with biblical views of sex outside of marriage, but you're certainly aware of the problems it's causing in our society.

## REASONS FOR SEXUAL INTEGRITY
*Instruction in sex is as important as instruction in food; yet not only are our adolescents not taught the physiology of sex, but never warned that the strongest sexual attraction may exist between persons so incompatible in*

*tastes and capacities that they could not endure living together for a week much less a lifetime.* (George Bernard Shaw)

There are three basic reasons behind my conclusion that even sex before marriage is a bad idea, which I'll tackle in order: it impacts our relationships, it can have physical consequences, and it goes against God's plan.

## EMOTIONAL CONSEQUENCES

I think the popular media do us a real disservice in this area. In many romantic comedies or dramas these days, a natural part of building any romantic relationship is sleeping together. And those movies and television shows are very effective, creating an emotional connection between the viewers and the characters so that we're actually happy for the on-screen lovers when it happens.

The reality is something quite different. Because of its intimacy—or what should be its intimacy—sex can negatively impact a relationship that might otherwise have had a chance to grow into a solid friendship and possibly a marriage. And that should be the goal of dating: friendship, and then, when you've found your soul mate, marriage.

Wise, godly men don't want to sabotage the potential of a relationship or future ones for a few moments of pleasure. Being a true man today means learning to defer gratification.

As George Bernard Shaw's quote at the beginning of the article reminds us, sex does not assure that two people will grow closer together. Too often with young people, unfortunately, it only masks other problems in the relationship.

## PHYSICAL CONSEQUENCES

Sex outside of marriage creates another problem for today's men: the issue of absentee fathers. Until you are married and ready to be a father, you are taking a chance that you'll end up being one of those dads who sends support payments and struggles to find quality time with his child. Sure, there are ways to be careful, but why take the chance? Only one method is foolproof and accident-proof: just don't do it.

Consequences involve more than just pregnancy. Sex outside of marriage has always involved health risks for both partners. We started with syphilis and gonorrhea in my dad's era, added herpes in my time, and now face the challenges of HIV. What's next? We don't know, but history tells us there will surely be something new and more devastating in the area of sexually transmitted diseases.

## SPIRITUAL CONSEQUENCES

We hear a great deal of talk that girls should stay sexually pure so they can wear white on their wedding day. Why isn't there the same focus on boys staying pure? For some reason, there is a stigma on women who have a lot of sexual partners, but society seems to look at it differently when it comes to men. We've allowed ourselves to be fooled into thinking that it's acceptable because "that's what men do."

The Bible tells us to "run from sexual sin!" No other sin so clearly affects the body as this one does. "Sexual immorality is a sin against your own body" (1 Corinthians 6:18, paraphrase).

God created you. Your body is valuable. Don't be casual in what you do with it—don't give it away.

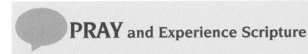

# PRAY and Experience Scripture

*If we confess our sins, He is faithful and righteous to forgive us our sins and to cleanse us from all unrighteousness.* (1 John 1:9 NASB)

As you reflect on your growing-up years and now into your adult life, ask God to bring to your mind any ways in which you may have hurt others, your relationship with the Lord, and your story of faith through compromising your sexual integrity.

*Heavenly Father, bring to my mind areas I need to confess and seek Your forgiveness. Show me any things I need to confess. I want to stand before you clean and forgiven. I want to live a life of sexual integrity. Show me, Lord. I am listening.*

Now confess anything the Lord reveals. Here's what a good confession sounds like:

*Jesus, I know it was wrong to...*

*I know that my sin hurt You because...*

*I know that my sin hurt others/my testimony of faith because...*

*Will you forgive me?*

Now rejoice gratefully in His promised forgiveness as you claim the promise of 1 John 1:9.

## Guard Your Mind

Finally, be vigilant with your thoughts and what goes into your mind (Matthew 6:22–23). Pornography is one of the largest industries on the Internet, which makes it easy for men to bring it right into their homes, where it will quickly gain a foothold if we aren't careful. Whether it creeps in through magazines, television, or the computer, the best way to avoid an addiction to pornography is to avoid the stuff altogether.

Addiction to pornography is just as real as an addiction to alcohol or other drugs, and it can be just as damaging. Like other addictions, it often starts in a subtle way. You don't have to find yourself at an adult bookstore or an X-rated movie to be tempted or led down the path. Today, there are so many avenues where we might find ourselves confronted with those impure thoughts. And even if we think we are mature enough to recognize them and filter them out, what about our kids? If we put the *Sports Illustrated* swimsuit issue on the coffee table, what message are we imprinting on a twelve-year-old's mind?

As with any other addictive substance, you can't be too careful with sexually explicit materials. The next time you're tempted to look, keep this in mind: I have friends who are involved in organizations that are trying to combat the global epidemic of human trafficking. They tell me there's a good chance that the person you're staring at is quite likely a runaway or slave, and that sultry smile is probably forced, hiding a life of incredible pain and hopelessness. Just don't go there.

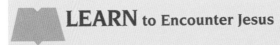

## LEARN to Encounter Jesus

*He is intimate with the upright.* (Proverbs 3:32 NASB)

Pornography makes a promise of closeness and intimacy, a promise that can never be fulfilled. Jesus makes a promise of intimacy that's certain. Proverbs tells us that the Lord has an intimacy and closeness with the upright. The "upright" are those individuals who yield to what God reveals about Himself. Remember how Jesus declared that He calls His followers "friends" (John 15:15)? Your friend Jesus desires intimacy with you.

Pause now to pray. Tell Jesus that you want to be closer to Him—and want the true intimacy that He can provide.

*Dear Jesus, please deepen my intimacy and friendship with You. I want the true closeness of relationship that You can provide. I need to be closer to You because... Talk to me as Your friend. Tell me more about You.*

### DARE TO BE DIFFERENT

It takes a strong man to be willing to follow this path of sexual purity, a much stronger man than the one who takes the easy way out and acts on what feels good at the time. If your convictions are that you shouldn't have sex outside of marriage, you're going to face a lot of questions, sometimes even ridicule. It takes a very strong man today to hold up under that kind of pressure.

Now, if we do believe that sex outside of marriage and viewing pornography are wrong or harmful, we've got to teach our boys and girls to see that as well—even if we once did it. I wonder if some fathers are hesitant to talk about this because they feel they don't have the credibility to do so. Maybe their backgrounds include sex outside of marriage, or maybe they're still stumbling with their own thought lives today. If this is the case for you, use those struggles and the lessons you've learned along the way to teach your children and help them avoid making poor choices. For example, a father may have smoked cigarettes at one time, but then realized they can cause lung cancer, so he quit. He wouldn't then turn around and let his children smoke just because he once made the same mistake.

If you aren't yet married, focus on positive relationships grounded in friendship, and stand firm in the knowledge that you are man enough without notches in your bedpost. There are too many reasons to wait. And being willing to be evaluated on a different scorecard is part of being a man!

 **SHARE** with Others in Community

*And let us consider how we may spur one another on toward love and good deeds.* (Hebrews 10:24 NIV)

Take a moment to reflect on a person or small group of men who could provide some of the encouragement that the writer of Hebrews is suggesting. You need men in your life who can "spur you on to love and good deeds"! Who is that person or small group?

Decide who you might talk to about your commitment and/or struggle with sexual integrity. Talk and pray together with this prayer partner or small group.

✝ *Jesus, change me so that I can live a life of sexual integrity. I want to experience deepened love with You and true closeness in the relationships You have provided. Empower me by Your Spirit to live uprightly with You, expressing a life of purity and righteousness to my family, friends, and others around me.*

#  LOVE Others in Community

Look for opportunities to talk with other men about your commitment to sexual integrity and the reasons behind your decision. Your words might begin with:

*It is hard to live a life of purity, but I'm committed to do that because Jesus has...*

# 20

## THE CULTURE-WISE FAMILY
From *The Culture-Wise Family*
by Ted Baehr and Pat Boone

### JESUS, RESET MY FAMILY LEGACY
*Jesus, help me to lead my family in a way
that protects my family from the moral decline
of our culture. At the same time, I want to lead
my family in how to stand up for the things
that are important to You.*

## PREFACE

The late intellectual and humorist Steve Allen once explained why tolerance is not always an option for Christians. He asked his audience, "If you came upon a burning bush where it was clear that God Himself was speaking to you, and the event was so frightening that you fell on your face before Him, and God told you exactly what judgment you faced if you refused to obey Him, what would you do?" You would do it, because not all choices are just a matter of opinion. You would obey because you had an experience that was true with the God who is Truth. And absolute truth sets us free (John 8:32).

God loves the world, not just the individuals in it (Romans 8:20–23). Those of the Christ Transforming Culture tradition view culture as a distinct, though related, part of Christ's universal reign. And although human activity can never bring salvation, Christian men and women bring a certain transforming element to our world as they live out their callings in distinction and honor, serving both as light that attracts non-Christians to the gospel and as salt that preserves society by bringing civil righteousness, justice, and compassion to bear on human relationships.

 **LEARN** to Encounter Jesus

*We have placed our confidence in him, and he will continue to rescue us. And you are helping us by praying for us.* (2 Corinthians 1:10–11 NLT)

Reflect on the state of our culture. What do you see in your community, neighborhood, or our country that indicates a need for Jesus?

*I see a need for Jesus to reset our culture, because all around me, I see...*

Now listen to the Lord's voice as He gives reassurance and hope: *Dear friend, I see the same needs that you do. The struggles of your community have not gone unnoticed. Rest assured. You can place your confidence in Me. I will continue to rescue you and those around you. Pray to Me for help. Join Me and let's change your world together.*

Now, consider your opportunities as a father to lead your family in transforming a culture. How might God want you and your family to live as "salt and light" in your community?

*I sense God would want me and my family to act as "salt" in our community by preserving...*

*I sense God would want our family to act as "light" in a dark world as we...*

## GOD IS THE MOST POWERFUL FORCE IN THE WORLD TODAY

Too many moral Americans believe we are facing overwhelming odds and unassailable power. Paul Klein, former vice president of NBC, said, "Television is the most powerful force in the world today."

Not even close. Television, nuclear power, communism, capitalism, the United States, sin, Satan, man, and all other powers combined pale in importance and shadowy insignificance when compared to the power of God: "Through him all things were made; without him nothing was made that has been made" (John 1:3).

Not only is God the most powerful force in the universe, but Jesus is the answer. He alone can deliver us from sin and death. God also tells us that, "Now you are the body of Christ, and members in particular" (1 Corinthians 12:27 KJV). And He affirms that, thanks to Jesus Christ's victory on the cross, "We are more than conquerors through him who loved us" (Romans 8:37).

Therefore, we can confidently respond to His instructions by standing in the whole armor of God against the wiles of the adversary—including immoral media. We not only have every right to unite to oppose evil in our world, but we are called to and have the power to rebuke such evil in the love of Christ.

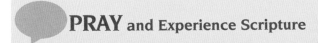

## PRAY and Experience Scripture

*Sanctify them by the truth; your word is truth.* (John 17:17 NIV)

In order for us to stand strong against the wiles of the adversary and the evil of our world, we must be able to accurately handle the sword of the Spirit—the Word of God (Ephesians 6:17). Read through the declarations of Psalm 119 below. Reflect on each verse and ask the Holy Spirit to show you the verse that needs to be more real in your life so that you and your family can be a part of transforming the culture. Ask the Lord to sanctify you with His Word.

- "I have hidden your word in my heart" (v. 11)
- "I have recited aloud all the laws you have given us." (v. 13)
- "I have rejoiced in your decrees as much as riches." (v. 14)
- "I will study your commandments and reflect upon your ways." (v. 15)
- "I will delight in your statutes and not forget your Word." (v. 16)
- "I need the guidance of your commands." (v. 19)
- "I am overwhelmed continually with a desire for your laws." (v. 20)

Which of these declarations needs to be more true of your life as you seek to lead your family and stand against the darkness of our world? Ask the Holy Spirit to use His truth to transform your life, family, and the world around you.

*Jesus, I sense it would be important for me to* _____
*because I know that we need You to reset and transform…*

## MAKE A DIFFERENCE

We must care enough about God and our neighbors to communicate His gospel with power and take every thought captive for Christ. We must learn the principles of powerful communication so that we can communicate the gospel through the mass media to reach every man, woman, and child with biblical truth.

Furthermore, we must redeem the culture so that the good, the true, and the beautiful—not vain imaginations—are proclaimed throughout the world. In obedience to His written Word, Christians need to reclaim the culture for Christ by advancing on several fronts:

- We need to raise the consciousness of Christians to impact the culture.
- We need to witness to and disciple everyone.
- We need to produce quality mass media of entertainment, art, and culture.

So how can you make a difference? Choose to become informed about what is happening in Hollywood and the media. Spend your entertainment dollars wisely. Remember that every time you buy a movie ticket or other entertainment, it is a vote to the entertainment industry to make more of the same. Cast an informed vote. Also, voice your concerns to those responsible. Write to producers, distributors, and sponsors. The only way they will know your objections is if you tell them. Finally, actively participate in rejection of companies who act contrary to our biblical beliefs.

## SIGNS OF REVIVAL

The great missionary and explorer Dr. Livingstone left England for Africa at a young age to bring the gospel to the whole continent and to deliver the people of Africa from the slave trade. He preached every day for years with little success. He suffered malaria attacks more than sixty times and lost the use of one of his arms to a lion while rescuing a friend. Then he disappeared into the uncharted jungle.

A brash *New York Herald* reporter named Stanley was sent to find Dr. Livingstone. After one year, by the grace of God, he found Livingstone being cared for by the slave traders he had come to destroy. While on his deathbed, Livingstone introduced the reporter to Jesus Christ.

It was Stanley's articles that opened up Africa to the missionaries, and within three years, the king of England signed an edict abolishing the slave trade. All Livingstone had set out to do was accomplished, but first he had to become the humble man of character who could serve as a vessel for the pure gospel of Jesus Christ. In a similar manner, we must first submit to Christ before we can reach the world with the good news of His salvation. Let us all pray that we are on God's side and that He does His will in and through us to the honor and glory of His holy name.

# SHARE with Others in Community

*But we all, with unveiled face, beholding as in a mirror the glory of the Lord, are being transformed into the same image from glory to glory, just as from the Lord, the Spirit.* (2 Corinthians 3:18 NASB)

It's only Christ and Christ in us that transforms. Pause to consider:

*In order to better express Christ to my family and those around me, I need to become more* _____ *and less* _____.

Share your areas of needed change with a prayer partner or your small group. Allow others to pray with you and for you that these changes become true in your life. Give Him praise that His Spirit is bringing Christlikeness to your life!

*I am hopeful that God is going to change me/my* _____ *by* _____.

 # LOVE Others in Community

Look for an opportunity to get involved in a specific community effort. Look for a cause that will allow you and your family to stand up for the values that honor Jesus. As you talk with others, voice your claims for Christ and the things

He loves rather than giving voice to what you're against. Your words might begin with these:

*I'm grateful to be involved in* _____, *because Jesus has given me a special love for* _____, *and I want to do my part.*

# *Appendix*

## ABOUT THE AUTHORS
## AND THEIR RESOURCES

**TED BAEHR AND PAT BOONE**

Excerpt from: **The Culture-Wise Family: Upholding Christian Values in a Mass Media World**

Publisher: Baker Books

ISBN: 0801017327

Copyright © Ted Baehr and Pat Boone

To buy the complete book, go to www.bakerbookstore.com

### About the Authors:

**Pat Boone** was second only to Elvis in the 1950s and early 1960s as the most popular singer of that decade. In his trademark white buckshoes, Boone skyrocketed to fame with hits such as "Two Hearts," "Ain't That a Shame," and "Letters in the Sand." He appeared in fifteen films and hosted his own televisions series for three years. In the 60s and 70s the Boone family toured as gospel singers and recorded gospel albums, such as *The Pat Boone Family* and *The Family Who Prays*. Pat and his wife, Shirley, have four daughters: Cherry, Lindy, Debby, and Laury.

**Ted Baehr** is founder and publisher of MOVIEGUIDE®: The Family Guide to Movies and Entertainment and chairman of the Christian Film & Television Commission® ministry, as well as a noted critic, educator, lecturer, and media pundit. His life's purpose is to be used of God to redeem the values of the media while educating audiences on how to use discernment in selecting their entertainment.

• • • • •

CAREY CASEY
Excerpt from: **Championship Fathering**
Publisher: Tyndale House Publishers
ISBN: 1589975340
Copyright © Carey Casey
To buy the complete book and other resources, go to www.fathers.com

ABOUT THE AUTHOR:

**Carey Casey** is CEO of the National Center for Fathering and a dynamic speaker, inspiring audiences with a call to Championship Fathering. He's known as a compassionate ambassador, particularly within the American sports community. He is also general editor of *The 21-Day Dad's Challenge: Three Weeks to a Better Relationship With Your Kids* (2011). Since 2009, Carey has served on the White House Task Force on Fatherhood and Healthy Families. He also serves as a member of the executive committee of the National Fatherhood Leaders Group, which promotes responsible fatherhood policy, research, advocacy, and practice. For more information, go to www.fathers.com.

• • • • •

JIM DALY
Excerpt from: **The Good Dad: Becoming the Father You Were Meant to Be**
Used by permission of Zondervan. www.zondervan.com
ISBN: 031033179X
Copyright © 2014 by James Daly
To buy the complete book, go to www.family.christianbook.com

ABOUT THE AUTHOR:

**Jim Daly**, president and CEO of Focus on the Family, has received the World Children's Center Humanitarian Award and the Children's Hunger Fund Children's Champion Award. He has appeared on ABC's *World News Tonight* and PBS's *Religion and Ethics*. He was featured in *Time*, *The Wall Street Journal*, *The New York Times*, and *Newsweek*, which named him a top 10 next-generation evangelical leader of influence. Daly and his wife have two sons and reside in Colorado Springs. Visit www.focusonthefamily.com.

• • • • •

**TAMMY DAUGHTRY**

Original article by Tammy Daughtry: **"Divorced and Still a Much-Loved Dad"**

Contact Tammy at www.coparentinginternational.com

ABOUT THE AUTHOR:

**Tammy Bennett-Daughtry** is the founder and CEO of CoParenting International, launched in January 2004 as a resource to address the critical impact of coparenting on children of divorce. Since 2004, coparenting seminars, evening classes, e-newsletters, and one-on-one sessions have helped change thousands of lives. She is an author and dynamic public speaker and has a strong entrepreneur mind-set. Tammy holds events in local churches, YMCAs, and various venues around the country.

• • • • •

**BARBARA DOYLE**

Original article by Barbara Doyle: **"Training Children To Honor Their Fathers"**

Contact Barbara at www.ironsharpensiron.net

ABOUT THE AUTHOR:

**Barb Doyle** is a fully devoted Christ follower who longs to help others become the same. She came to faith through the collegiate ministry of The Navigators, where she learned to reproduce her life. Barb loves God's Word and loves to invest time studying and learning God's ways. She has been married to her husband, Brian, since 1987 and is the mother of five wonderful children. Discipling Jessica, Michael, Matthew, Tim, and Susie is Barb's first ministry and together with her husband has home educated the children. She supports Brian in his role as a national leader with Iron Sharpens Iron and speaks at national women's conferences. Barb's roots are in New England, but she and her family currently reside in Central Florida.

• • • • •

BRIAN DOYLE
Original article by Brian Doyle: **"From Obey to Honor"**
Contact Brian at www.ironsharpensiron.net

ABOUT THE AUTHOR:
**Brian Doyle** is passionate to see churches equip men for spiritual leadership in the home, church, and community. He has served with The Navigators on campuses and military bases as well as on staff with Promise Keepers in the 1990s. He now serves as founder and president of Iron Sharpens Iron, which equips churches to train men for spiritual leadership. He oversees the Iron Sharpens Iron Conference Network, which has hosted equipping conferences for men around the nation since 2001. These conferences are the most visible part of the regional ministries that equip churches to reach and build godly men. Brian also serves on the board of directors of The Fatherhood Commission and on the executive board of the National Coalition of Men's Ministries. Brian and his wife, Barbara, consider it a privilege to disciple their five children to follow Jesus Christ.

• • • • •

TONY DUNGY WITH NATHAN WHITAKER
Excerpt from: **Uncommon Man: Finding Your Path to Significance**
Publisher: Tyndale Momentum
ISBN: 1414326823
Copyright © 2009, 2011 Tony Dungy
To buy the complete book, go to www.christianbooks.com

ABOUT THE AUTHOR:
**Tony Dungy** is the number-one New York Times best-selling author of Quiet Strength, Uncommon, and The Mentor Leader. He led the Indianapolis Colts to Super Bowl victory on February 4, 2007, the first such win for an African-American head coach. Dungy established another NFL first by becoming the first head coach to lead his teams to the playoffs for ten consecutive years. Dungy has been involved in a wide variety of charitable organizations, including All Pro Dad. He retired from coaching in 2009 and now serves as a studio analyst for NBC's Football Night in America. He and his wife, Lauren, have been married for thirty-one years and are the parents of nine children. For more information, go to www.allprodad.com.

## DENNIS GALLAHER
Original article by Dennis Gallaher: **"Remembering Dad"**
Contact Dennis at www.freedomnb.org

ABOUT THE AUTHOR:

**Dennis Gallaher** and his wife, Jan, have been caring for God's people for thirty-seven years, the past twenty-seven years at Freedom Fellowship Church. They have two grown sons and four grandchildren. Dennis has a degree in ministry from Hill Country Bible College, a BA in biblical counseling from Trinity College, and a MA in professional counseling from Texas State University. In their heart of hearts, they are committed to shepherding God's people and loving His church with sincerity and dedication. You can read Dennis' blogs at www.dennisgallaher.com and at www.actlikemenblog.com.

• • • • •

## NICK HALL
Original article by Nick Hall: **"Jesus Resets Families"**
Contact Nick at www.pulsemovement.com

ABOUT THE AUTHOR:

**Nick Hall** is the founder and chief communicator of PULSE, a nonprofit organization at the center of the largest student-led prayer and outreach efforts in America today. Launched through an English paper Nick wrote as a junior at North Dakota State University, the PULSE movement has grown to impact more than thirty university campuses and more than 250,000 people each year. PULSE exists to awaken culture to the reality of Jesus. Nick has played a role in equipping tens of thousands of students while impacting more than a million people with the life-giving message of Jesus. He is married to his best friend, Tiffany. When they are not on the road, they make their home in the Twin Cities of Minneapolis-St. Paul.

• • • • •

JADE LEE

Original article by Jade Lee: **"Honoring the Real God to Honor Your Father"**

Contact Jade at www.jadelee.org

ABOUT THE AUTHOR:

**Jade Lee** serves as the CEO of JadeLee.org, which provides resources for pastors, laypersons, and local communities. JLO also hosts annual community-boosting events that stimulate economic growth and job opportunities such as career fairs, business expos, beauty fairs, and the JLO Women's Leadership Academy. Jade and her husband, Corey, copastor The Convergence Church in Atlanta, Georgia, where they minister weekly to hundreds of students and young adults. Jade is author of *Free To Be You*, *The Pull*, and the Women of the Bible Series.

• • • • •

JOSH MCDOWELL

Excerpt from: **The Father Connection**

Publisher: B&H Publishers. Used by Permission.

Copyright © Josh McDowell Ministry. All rights reserved.

To order the complete book, go to www.josh.org

ABOUT THE AUTHOR:

**Josh McDowell** has been reaching the spiritually skeptical for more than five decades. Josh has spoken to more than 25 million people in 128 countries. He is the author or coauthor of 148 books, with over 51 million copies distributed worldwide, including *Straight Talk with Your Kids About Sex*, *Experience Your Bible*, *Evidence for the Historical Jesus*, *More Than a Carpenter* (over 15 million copies printed in 85 languages), and *The New Evidence That Demands a Verdict*, recognized by *World* magazine as one of the twentieth century's top 40 books. Josh continues to travel throughout the United States and countries around the world, helping young people and adults strengthen their faith and understanding of Scripture. Josh will tell you that his family is his ministry. He and his wife, Dottie, have been married for more than forty years and have four children and numerous grandchildren.

• • • • •

## DENNIS RAINEY

Excerpt from: **The Forgotten Commandment**, originally published as *The Tribute* and *The Tribute and The Promise*

Publisher: FamilyLife® Publishing (April, 2014)

Copyright © Dennis Rainey, 1994

To buy the complete book, go to www.shop.familylife.com

ABOUT THE AUTHOR:

**Dennis Rainey** is the president and CEO of FamilyLife, a subsidiary of Campus Crusade for Christ. Since the organization began in 1976, Dennis' leadership has enabled FamilyLife to grow into a dynamic and vital ministry that offers families blueprints for living godly lives. Dennis has authored or coauthored more than two dozen books including the best-selling *Moments Together for Couples* and *Staying Close*. Dennis and Barbara have been married since 1972 and love laughing with their six children and numerous grandchildren. For more information, go to www.familylife.com.

· · · · ·

## SAMUEL RODRIGUEZ

Excerpt from: **The Lamb's Agenda: Why Jesus Is Calling You to a Life of Righteousness and Justice**

Used by permission of Thomas Nelson – www.thomasnelson.com

ISBN: 1400204496

Copyright © 2013 Samuel Rodriguez

To buy the complete book in English or Spanish and to get other resources, go to www.christianbooks.com

ABOUT THE AUTHOR:

**Rev. Samuel Rodriguez** is president of the National Hispanic Christian Leadership Conference, America's largest Hispanic Christian organization. Named by CNN as "The leader of the Hispanic Evangelical Movement" and by the *San Francisco Chronicle* as one of America's new evangelical leaders, Rodriguez is also the recipient of the Martin Luther King Jr. Award presented by the Congress on Racial Equality. A featured speaker in White House and congressional meetings, he has been featured, profiled, and quoted by such media outlets as *The New York Times*, *Christianity Today*, *The Washington Post*, *The Wall Street Journal*, *Newsweek*, *Univision*, *Fox News*, *Time*, and *Ministries Today*. Rodriguez is also the senior pastor of New Season Christian Worship Center in Sacramento, California. For more information, go to www.nhclc.org.

JOHN TRENT & GARY SMALLEY

Excerpt from: *The Blessing: Giving the Gift of Unconditional Love and Acceptance*

Used by permission of Thomas Nelson – www.thomasnelson.com
ISBN: 0849946379
Copyright © 1993 John Trent and Gary Smalley
The complete book and related resources are available at: www.family.christianbook.com

ABOUT THE AUTHOR:

**Gary Smalley** is one of America's foremost experts on marriage and family relationships. Dr. John Trent is president of Encouraging Words, an outreach program committed to strengthening relationships worldwide. Together, these counselors make a highly effective team in keeping spouses, siblings, children, and friends together—for the long term. Between them they've authored more than twenty books, and many of the ones they've written together have been award-winning bestsellers. *The Gift of the Blessing* (formerly *The Blessing*) won the Gold Medallion award for excellence in Christian publishing. This book was—and is—a source of emotional healing for those who never felt loved and accepted by their family, who never experienced "the blessing" of heartfelt affirmation. For information, go to www.theblessing.com.

• • • • •

TODD STRAWSER

Original article by Todd Strawser: **"Honor as the Priority"**

Contact Todd at www.christianfamilyeldercare.org

ABOUT THE AUTHOR:

In addition to raising their seven children, Todd and his wife, Jessica, direct the Christian Family Eldercare, a national network dedicated to encouraging, equipping, and enabling relationship-centered eldercare. Todd works as an IT project manager in Colorado Springs and runs a small property management business. Todd and his family share a deep conviction to see the gospel of Christ advance and for the Christian church and family to thrive. Todd's passion is to see ministry leaders bolstered to serve the church and glorify God in daily ministry to the saints.

• • • • •

## MITCH TEMPLE

Original article by Mitch Temple: **"My Tribute"**

Contact Mitch at www.fatherhoodcomission.com

ABOUT THE AUTHOR:

**Mitch Temple** has more than twenty-five years of experience in the church and nonprofit world. He is the author/coauthor of five books, speaks nationally and internationally, and serves as a consultant to the Christian film industry as well as churches, nonprofits, and secular organizations. Mitch is a licensed marriage and family therapist and former director of marriage and family at Focus on the Family. Mitch is one of the cofounders of The Fatherhood CoMission and is extremely passionate about helping churches and communities build up fathers.

• • • • •

## JOHN K. VINING

Excerpt from: *Family Ministry Frameworks: A Comprehensive Guide for Building Relational Ministry*

Publisher: Relationship Press

Copyright © 2003 John Kie Vining

ABOUT THE AUTHOR:

**John Vining** serves as clinical director for the Center for Relational Health in Cleveland, Tennessee, where he leads a team of professionals who serve the families of Southeastern Tennessee. As an ordained bishop within the Church of God, John has pastored at the local church level and provided direction to the entire denomination in the area of marriage and family ministry. Because of his burden for the health of ministry families, John and his wife, Su, currently serve alongside the Great Commandment Network leading retreats for pastors and their spouses. John has authored or coauthored more than twenty resources, including *Home Is Where the Hurt Is* and *Becoming Childwise*. To contact John, go to www.ycscleveland.com.

• • • • •

## ROLAND WARREN

Excerpt from: *Bad Dads of the Bible: 8 Mistakes Every Good Dad Can Avoid*
Used by permission of Zondervan – www.zondervan.com
ISBN: 031033716X
Copyright © 2014 Roland Warren
To buy the complete book, go to www.zondervan.com

ABOUT THE AUTHOR:

**Roland C. Warren** is the president and CEO of Care Net. Prior to his tenure at Care Net, Roland served as president of the National Fatherhood Initiative (NFI), where he was dedicated to the mission of improving the well-being of children by increasing the proportion of children that are raised with involved, responsible, and committed fathers. Roland is an inspirational servant leader with a heart for Christ and a mind for business. After twenty years in the corporate world (with IBM, Pepsi, and Goldman Sachs), Roland spent eleven years as president of National Fatherhood Initiative before joining Care Net as president and CEO. For more information, go to www.care-net.org.

• • • • •

## MARK L. WILLIAMS

Excerpt from: *The Praying Church Handbook* volume II (with P. Douglas Small)
Publisher: Alive Publications – www.alivepublications.org
Contact Mark at www.churchofgod.org

ABOUT THE AUTHOR:

**Dr. Mark L. Williams** serves as general overseer for the Church of God, the highest leadership role in the denomination. Elected to the post in 2012, Williams previously served as second assistant general overseer from 2008 to 2012. Prior to leading the Church of God on the Executive Committee, Williams was state overseer for California-Nevada and was a member of the International Executive Council. Williams began his ministerial career as an evangelist, traveling on the weekends while earning a degree from Lee University.

• • • • •

## BILLY WILSON

Excerpt from: **Father Cry: Healing Your Heart and the Hearts of Those You Love**
Publisher: Chosen, a Division of Baker Publishing Group
Copyright © 2012 William M. Wilson
To buy the complete book, go to www.christianbook.com

### ABOUT THE AUTHOR:

**Billy Wilson** is president of Oral Roberts University and has more than thirty-two years of ministry experience. In that time he has served in many roles and personally ministered in more than eighty nations. The author of numerous articles, sermon series, video projects, and books, Wilson has served as an influential leader in Spirit-empowered organizations, including Azusa Street Centennial, Empowered21, and more. He and his wife, Lisa, live in Tulsa, Oklahoma. For more information, contact the office of the president at www.oru.edu.

# ABOUT THE GREAT COMMANDMENT NETWORK

**The Great Commandment Network** is an international collaborative network of strategic kingdom leaders from the faith community, marketplace, education, and caregiving fields who prioritize the powerful simplicity of the words of Jesus to love God, love others, and see others become His followers (Matthew 22:37–40, Matthew 28:19–20).

THE GREAT COMMANDMENT NETWORK IS SERVED THROUGH THE FOLLOWING:

**Relationship Press** – This team collaborates, supports, and joins together with churches, denominational partners, and professional associates to develop, print, and produce resources that facilitate ongoing Great Commandment ministry.

**The Center for Relational Leadership** – Their mission is to teach, train, and mentor both ministry and corporate leaders in Great Commandment principles, seeking to equip leaders with relational skills so they might lead as Jesus led.

**The Galatians 6:6 Retreat Ministry** – This ministry offers a unique two-day retreat for ministers and their spouses for personal renewal and for reestablishing and affirming ministry and family priorities.

**The Center for Relational Care** (CRC) – The CRC provides therapy and support to relationships in crisis through an accelerated process of growth and healing, including Relational Care Intensives for couples, families, and singles.

For more information on how you, your church, ministry, denomination, or movement can be served by the Great Commandment Network write or call:

**Great Commandment Network**
**2511 South Lakeline Blvd.**
**Cedar Park, Texas 78613**
**#800-881-8008**
Or visit our website: www.GreatCommandment.net

# A SPIRIT-EMPOWERED FAITH
## Expresses Itself in Great Commission Living
## Empowered by Great Commandment Love

 **begins with the end in mind:**
**The Great Commission calls us**
**to make disciples.**

*"Therefore, go and make disciples of all the nations, baptizing them in*
*the name of the Father and the Son and the Holy Spirit. Teach these new*
*disciples to obey all the commands I have given you. And be sure of this:*
*I am with you always, even to the end of the age."* (Matthew 28:19–20)

The ultimate goal of our faith journey is to relate to the person of Jesus, because it is our relational connection to Jesus that will produce Christ-likeness and spiritual growth. This relational perspective of discipleship is required if we hope to have a faith that is marked by the Spirit's power.

Models of discipleship that are based solely upon what we *know* and what we *do* are incomplete, lacking the empowerment of a life of loving and living intimately with Jesus. **A Spirit-empowered faith is relational and impossible to realize apart from a special work of the Spirit.** For example, the Spirit-empowered outcome of "listening to and hearing God" implies relationship—it is both relational in focus and requires the Holy Spirit's power to live.

 **begins at the right place:**
**The Great Commandment calls us to**
**start with loving God and loving others.**

*"'You must love the Lord your God with all your heart, all your soul,*
*and all your mind.' This is the first and greatest commandment.*
*A second is equally important: 'Love your neighbor as yourself.'*
*The entire law and all the demands of the prophets are*
*based on these two commandments."* (Matthew 22:37–40)

Relevant discipleship does not begin with doctrines or teaching, parables or stewardship—but with loving the Lord with all your heart, mind, soul, and strength and then loving the people closest to you. Since Matthew 22:37–40 gives us the first and greatest commandment, *a Spirit-empowered faith starts where the Great Commandment tells us to start: A disciple must first learn to deeply love the Lord and to express His love to the "nearest ones"—his or her family, church, and community (and in that order).*

 embraces a relational process of Christlikeness.

**Scripture reminds us that there are three sources of light for our journey: Jesus, His Word, and His people. The process of discipleship (or becoming more like Jesus) occurs as we relate intimately with each source of light.**

*"Walk in the light while you can, so the darkness will not overtake you."*
(John 12:35)

Spirit-empowered discipleship will require a lifestyle of:
- Fresh encounters with Jesus (John 8:12)
- Frequent experiences of Scripture (Psalm 119:105)
- Faithful engagement with God's people (Matthew 5:14)

 **can be defined with observable outcomes using a biblical framework.**

**The metrics for measuring Spirit-empowered faith or the growth of a disciple come from Scripture and are organized/framed around four distinct dimensions of a disciple who serves.**

*Now these are the gifts Christ gave to the church: the apostles,*
*the prophets, the evangelists, and the pastors and teachers.*
*Their responsibility is to equip God's people to do his work and*
*build up the church, the body of Christ.*
(Ephesians 4:11–12)

A relational framework for organizing Spirit-Empowered Discipleship Outcomes draws from a cluster analysis of several Greek (*diakoneo, leitourgeo, douleuo*) and Hebrew words ('*abad, Sharat*) which elaborate on the Ephesians 4:12 declaration that Christ's followers are to be equipped for works of ministry or service. Therefore, the 40 Spirit-Empowered Faith Outcomes have been identified and organized around:

- Serving/loving the Lord – *While they were* **ministering** *to the Lord and fasting…* (Acts 13:2 NASB).[1]
- Serving/loving the Word – *But we will devote ourselves to prayer and to the* **ministry** *of the word* (Acts 6:4 NASB).[2]
- Serving/loving people – *…through love* **serve** *one another* (Galatians 5:13 NASB).[3]
- Serving/loving His mission – *Now all these things are from God, who reconciled us to Himself through Christ and gave us the* **ministry** *of reconciliation* (2 Corinthians 5:18 NASB).[4]

1 Ferguson, David L. *Great Commandment Principle*. Cedar Park, Texas: Relationship Press, 2013.
2 Ferguson, David L. *Relational Foundations*. Cedar Park, Texas: Relationship Press, 2004.
3 Ferguson, David L. *Relational Discipleship*. Cedar Park, Texas: Relationship Press, 2005.
4 "Spirit Empowered Outcomes," www.empowered21.com, Empowered 21 Global Council, http://empowered21.com/discipleship-materials/.

# A SPIRIT-EMPOWERED DISCIPLE LOVES THE LORD THROUGH

### L1. Practicing thanksgiving in all things

*Enter the gates with thanksgiving* (Ps. 100:4). *In everything give thanks* (I Th. 5:18). *As sorrowful, yet always rejoicing* (II Cor. 6:10).

### L2. Listening to and hearing God for direction and discernment

*"Speak, Lord, Your servant is listening"* (I Sam. 3:8–9). *Mary…listening to the Lord's word, seated at his feet* (Lk.10:38–42). *"Shall I not share with Abraham what I am about to do?"* (Gen. 18:17). *His anointing teaches you all things* (I Jn. 2:27).

### L3. Experiencing God as He really is through deepened intimacy with Him

*"Hear, O Israel: The Lord our God, the Lord is one. Love the Lord your God with all your heart and with all your soul and with all your strength"* (Deut. 6:4, 5). *Yet the Lord longs to be gracious to you; therefore he will rise up to show you compassion. For the Lord is a God of justice* (Is. 30:18). See also John 14:9.

### L4. Rejoicing regularly in my identity as "His Beloved"

*And His banner over me is love* (Song of Sol. 2:4). *To the praise of the glory of His grace, which He freely bestowed on us in the beloved* (Eph. 1:6). *For the Lord gives to His beloved even in their sleep* (Ps. 127:2).

### L5. Living with a passionate longing for purity and to please Him in all things

*Who may ascend the hill of the Lord—he who has clean hands and a pure heart* (Ps. 24:3, 4). *Beloved, let us cleanse ourselves from all of flesh and spirit, perfecting holiness in the fear of God* (II Cor. 7:1). *"I always do the things that are pleasing to Him"* (Jn. 8:29). *"Though He slay me, yet will I hope in Him"* (Job 13:15).

**L6.   Consistent practice of self-denial, fasting, and solitude rest**

*He turned and said to Peter, "Get behind me, Satan! You are an obstacle to me. You are thinking not as God does, but as human beings do"* (Matt. 16:23). *"But you when you fast…"* (Mt. 6:17). *"Be still and know that I am God" (Ps. 46:10).*

**L7.   Entering often into Spirit-led praise and worship**

*Bless the Lord O my soul and all that is within me…* (Ps. 103:1). *Worship the Lord with reverence* (Ps. 2:11). *I praise Thee O Father, Lord of heaven and earth…* (Mt. 11:25).

**L8.   Disciplined, bold, and believing prayer**

*Pray at all times in the Spirit* (Eph. 6:18). *"Call unto me and I will answer…"* (Jer. 33:3). *If you ask according to His will—He hears—and you will have…* (I Jn. 5:14–15).

**L9.   Yielding to the Spirit's fullness as life in the Spirit brings supernatural intimacy with the Lord, manifestation of divine gifts, and witness of the fruit of the Spirit**

*For by one Spirit we were all baptized into one body, whether Jews or Greeks, whether slaves or free, and we were all made to drink of one Spirit* (I Cor. 12:13). *"You shall receive power when the Holy Spirit comes upon you"* (Acts 1:8). *But to each one is given the manifestation of the Spirit for the common good* (I Cor. 12:7). See also I Pet. 4:10 and Rom. 12:6.

**L10.   Practicing the presence of the Lord, yielding to the Spirit's work of Christlikeness**

*And we who with unveiled faces all reflect the Lord's glory, are being transformed into His likeness from glory to glory which comes from the Lord, who is the Spirit* (II Cor. 3:18). *As the deer pants after the water brooks, so my soul pants after You, O God* (Ps. 42:1).

# A SPIRIT-EMPOWERED DISCIPLE LOVES THE WORD THROUGH

**W1. Frequently being led by the Spirit into deeper love for the One who wrote the Word**

*"Love the Lord thy God—love thy neighbor; upon these two commandments deepens all the law and prophets"* (Mt. 22:37-40). *I delight in Your commands because I love them* (Ps. 119:47). *"The ordinances of the Lord are pure—they are more precious than gold—sweeter than honey"* (Ps. 19:9-10).

**W2. Being a "living epistle" in reverence and awe as His Word becomes real in my life, vocation, and calling**

*You yourselves are our letter—known and read by all men* (II Cor. 3:2). *And the Word became flesh and dwelt among us* (Jn. 1:14). *Husbands love your wives—cleansing her by the washing with water through the Word* (Eph. 5:26). See also Tit. 2:5. *Whatever you do, do your work heartily, as for the Lord…* (Col. 3:23).

**W3. Yielding to the Scripture's protective cautions and transforming power to bring life change in me**

*I gain understanding from Your precepts; therefore I hate every wrong path* (Ps. 119:104). *"Be it done unto me according to Your word"* (Lk. 1:38). *How can a young man keep his way pure? By living according to Your word* (Ps. 119:9). See also Col. 3:16–17.

**W4. Humbly and vulnerably sharing of the Spirit's transforming work through the Word**

*I will speak of your statutes before kings and will not be put to shame* (Ps. 119:46). *Preach the word; be ready in season and out to shame* (II Tim. 4:2).

## W5.  Meditating consistently on more and more of the Word hidden in the heart

*I have hidden Your Word in my heart that I might not sin against You* (Ps. 119:12). *May the words of my mouth and the meditation of my heart be pleasing in Your sight, O Lord, my rock and my redeemer* (Ps. 19:14).

## W6.  Encountering Jesus in the Word for deepened transformation in Christlikeness

*All of us, gazing with unveiled face on the glory of the Lord, are being transformed into the same image from glory to glory, as from the Lord who is the Spirit* (II Cor. 3:18). *If you abide in Me and My words abide in you, ask whatever you wish, and it will be done for you* (Jn. 15:7). See also Lk. 24:32, Ps. 119:136, and II Cor. 1:20.

## W7.  A life explained as one of "experiencing Scripture"

*"This is that spoken of by the prophets"* (Acts 2:16). *My comfort in my suffering is this: Your promise preserves my life* (Ps. 119:50). *My soul is consumed with longing for Your laws at all times* (Ps. 119:20).

## W8.  Living "naturally supernatural" in all of life as His Spirit makes the written Word (*logos*) the living Word (*rhema*)

*Faith comes by hearing and hearing by the word* (rhema) *of Christ* (Rom. 10:17). *Your Word is a lamp to my feet and a light for my path* (Ps. 119:105).

## W9.  Living  abundantly "in the present" as His Word brings healing to hurt and anger, guilt, fear, and condemnation—which are *heart hindrances* to life abundant

*"The thief comes to steal, kill and destroy…"* (Jn 10:10). *I run in the path of Your commands for You have set my heart free* (Ps. 119:32). *And you shall know the truth and the truth shall set you free* (Jn. 8:32). *For freedom Christ set us free; so stand firm and do not submit again to the yoke of slavery* (Gal. 5:1).

**W10. Implicit, unwavering trust that His Word will never fail**
*"The grass withers and the flower fades but the word of God abides forever*
(Is. 40:8). *"So will My word be which goes forth from My mouth, it will not return
to me empty"* (Is. 55:11).

# A SPIRIT-EMPOWERED DISCIPLE
# LOVES PEOPLE THROUGH

**P1. Living a Spirit-led life of doing good in all of life: relationships and
vocation, community and calling**
*…He went about doing good…*(Acts 10:38). *"Let your light shine before men
in such a way that they may see your good works, and glorify your Father who
is in heaven"* (Mt. 5:16). *"But love your enemies, and do good, and lend, expecting nothing in return, and you reward will be great, and you will be sons of the
Most High; for He Himself is kind to ungrateful and evil men"* (Lk. 6:35). See
also Rom. 15:2.

**P2. "Startling people" with loving initiatives to "give first"**
*"Give, and it will be given to you. They will pour into your lap a good measure—
pressed down, shaken together, and running over. For by your standard of measure it will be measured to you in return"* (Lk. 6:38). *But Jesus was saying, "Father,
forgive them; for they do not know what they are doing"* (Lk. 23:34). See also Lk.
23:43 and Jn. 19:27.

**P3. Discerning the relational needs of others with a heart to give of His love**
*Let no unwholesome word proceed from your mouth, but only such a word as
is good for edification according to the need of the moment, so that it will give
grace to those who hear* (Eph. 4:29). *And my God will supply all your needs according to His riches in glory in Christ Jesus* (Phil. 4:19). See also Lk. 6:30.

**P4.  Seeing people as needing BOTH redemption from sin AND intimacy in relationships, addressing both human fallen-ness and aloneness**

*But God demonstrates His own love toward us, in that while we were yet sinners, Christ died for us* (Rom. 5:8). *When Jesus came to the place, He looked up and said to him, "Zaccheus, hurry and come down, for today I must stay at your house"* (Lk. 19:5). See also Mk. 8:24 and Gen. 2:18.

**P5.  Ministering His life and love to our nearest ones at home and with family as well as faithful engagement in His body, the church**

*You husbands in the same way, live with your wives in an understanding way, as with someone weaker, since she is a woman; and show her honor as a fellow heir of the grace of life, so that your prayers will not be hindered* (I Pet. 3:7). See also I Pet. 3:1 and Ps. 127:3.

**P6.  Expressing the fruit of the Spirit as a lifestyle and identity**

*But the fruit of the Spirit is love, joy, peace, patience, kindness, goodness, faithfulness, gentleness, self-control…* (Gal. 5:22-23). *With the fruit of a man's mouth his stomach will be satisfied; He will be satisfied with the product of his lips* (Prov. 18:20).

**P7.  Expecting and demonstrating the supernatural as His spiritual gifts are made manifest and His grace is at work by His Spirit**

*In the power of signs and wonders, in the power of the Spirit; so that from Jerusalem and round about as far as Illyricum I have fully preached the gospel of Christ* (Rom. 15:19). *"Truly, truly, I say to you, he who believes in Me, the works that I do, he will do also…"* (Jn. 14:12). See also I Cor. 14:1.

**P8.  Taking courageous initiative as a peacemaker, reconciling relationships along life's journey**

*…Live in peace with one another* (I Th. 5:13). *For He Himself is our peace, who made both groups into one and broke down the barrier of the dividing wall* (Eph. 2:14). *Therefore, confess your sins to one another, and pray for one another so that you may be healed* (Jas. 5:16).

**P9.  Demonstrating His love to an ever growing network of "others" as He continues to challenge us to love "beyond our comfort"**

*The one who says, "I have come to know Him," and does not keep His command-ments, is a liar, and the truth is not in him (I Jn. 2:4). If someone says, "I love God," and hates his brother, he is a liar; for the one who does not love his brother whom he has seen, cannot love God whom he has not seen (I Jn. 4:20).*

**P10.  Humbly acknowledging to the Lord, ourselves, and others that it is Jesus in and through us who is loving others at their point of need**

*"Take My yoke upon you and learn from Me, for I am gentle and humble in heart, and you will find rest for your souls" (Mt. 11:29). "If I then, the Lord and the Teach-er, washed your feet, you also ought to wash one another's feet" (Jn. 13:14).*

# A SPIRIT-EMPOWERED DISCIPLE LOVES HIS MISSION THROUGH

**M1.  Imparting the gospel and one's very life in daily activities and rela-tionships, vocation and community**

*Having so fond an affection for you, we were well-pleased to impart to you not only the gospel of God but also our own lives, because you had become very dear to us* (I Th. 2:8-9).  See also Eph. 6:19.

**M2.  Expressing and extending the kingdom of God as compassion, jus-tice, love, and forgiveness are shared**

*"I must preach the kingdom of God to the other cities also, for I was sent for this pur-pose" (Lk. 4:43). "As You sent Me into the world, I also have sent them into the world"* (Jn. 17:18). *Restore to me the joy of Your salvation and sustain me with a willing spirit. Then I will teach transgressors Your ways, and sinners will be converted to you* (Ps. 51:12–13). See also Mic. 6:8.

## M3. Championing Jesus as the only hope of eternal life and abundant living

*"There is no salvation through anyone else, nor is there any other name under heaven given to the human race by which we are to be saved"* (Acts 4:12). *"A thief comes only to steal and slaughter and destroy; I came so that they might have life and have it more abundantly"* (Jn. 10:10). See also Acts 4:12, Jn. 10:10, and Jn. 14:6.

## M4. Yielding to the Spirit's role to convict others as He chooses, resisting expressions of condemnation

*"And He, when He comes, will convict the world concerning sin and righteousness and judgment…"* (Jn. 16:8). *Who is the one who condemns? Christ Jesus is He who died, yes, rather who was raised, who is at the right hand of God, who also intercedes for us* (Rom. 8:34). See also Rom. 8:1.

## M5. Ministering His life and love to the "least of these"

*"Then He will answer them, 'Truly I say to you, to the extent that you did not do it to one of the least of these, you did not do it to Me'"* (Mt. 25:45). *Pure and undefiled religion in the sight of our God and Father is this: to visit orphans and widows in their distress, and to keep oneself unstained by the world* (Jas. 1:27).

## M6. Bearing witness of a confident peace and expectant hope in God's lordship in all things

*Now may the Lord of peace Himself continually grant you peace in every circumstance. The Lord be with you all!* (II Thess. 3:16). *Let the peace of Christ rule in your hearts, to which indeed you were called in one body; and be thankful* (Col. 3:15). See also Rom. 8:28 and Ps. 146:5.

## M7. Faithfully sharing of time, talent, gifts, and resources in furthering His mission

*Of this church I was made a minister according to the stewardship from God bestowed on me for your benefit, so that I might fully carry out the preaching of the word of God* (Col. 1:25). *"From everyone who has been given much, much will be required; and to whom they entrusted much, of him they will ask all the more"* (Lk. 12:48). See also I Cor. 4:1–2.

**M8.   Attentive listening to others' *story*, vulnerably sharing of our story, and a sensitive witness of Jesus' story as life's ultimate hope; developing your story of prodigal, preoccupied and pain-filled living; listening for others' story and sharing Jesus' story**

*"…But sanctify Christ as Lord in your hearts, always being ready to make a defense to everyone who asks you to give an account for the hope that is in you, yet with gentleness and reverence"* (I Pet. 3:15). *"…Because this son of mine was dead, and has come to life again"* (Luke 15:24). See also Mk. 5:21–42 and Jn. 9:1–35.

**M9.   Pouring our life into others, making disciples who in turn make disciples of others**

*"Go therefore and make disciples of all nations, baptizing them in the name of the Father and the Son and the Holy Spirit, teaching them to observe all that I commanded you; and lo, I am with you always, even to the end of the age"* (Mt. 28:19–20). See also II Tim. 2:2.

**M10.  Living submissively within His body, the church as instruction and encouragement, reproof and correction are graciously received by faithful disciples**

*…And be subject to one another in the fear of Christ* (Eph. 5:21). *Brethren, even if anyone is caught in any trespass, you who are spiritual, restore such a one in a spirit of gentleness; each one looking to yourself, so that you too will not be tempted* (Gal. 6:1). See also Gal. 6:2.

# Other Books
*in the*
# SPIRIT-EMPOWERED
*Faith*
## SERIES

PRAYING WITH *Jesus*

○ RESET
*My Prayer Life*

CRY OUT TO THE *Lord*

○ RESET
*My Walk with God*

**BroadStreet**
PUBLISHING

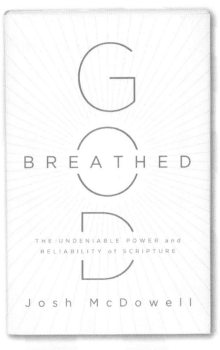

# TOGETHER

WASHINGTON, D.C. **7.16.16** NATIONAL MALL

Linking arms, lifting a unified sound asking
Jesus to reset our generation

# THE
# WORLD
# SEES
# DIVISION

—

BUT WE CAN CHANGE THAT

## JOIN THE CAMPAIGN
### RESET2016.COM

@JesusIsTheReset